Simplified **Grantwriting**

Simplified Grantwriting

Mary Ann Burke

CORWIN PRESS, INC.
A Sage Publications Company
Thousand Oaks, California

For information:

Corwin Press, Inc.
A Sage Publications Company
2455 Teller Road
Thousand Oaks, California 91320
www.corwinpress.com

Sage Publications Ltd.
6 Bonhill Street
London EC2A 4PU
United Kingdom

Sage Publications India Pvt. Ltd.
M-32 Market
Greater Kailash I
New Delhi 110 048 India

Printed in the United States of America

Library of Congress Cataloging-in-Publication Data

Burke, Mary Ann.
    Simplified grantwriting / by Mary Ann Burke.
        p. cm.
Includes bibliographical references and index.
ISBN 0-7619-4531-8 (c)
ISBN 0-7619-4532-6 (p)
1. Educational fundraising. 2. Proposal writing in education. 3.
Proposal writing for grants. I. Title.
    LC241 .B87 2002
        379.1'3—dc21   2002001003

This book is printed on acid-free paper.

02 03 04 05 10 9 8 7 6 5 4 3 2 1

Acquisitions Editor:	Robb Clouse
Editorial Assistant:	Erin Clow
Copy Editor:	Toni Williams
Production Editor:	Denise Santoyo
Typesetter:	Tina Hill
Indexer:	Kathy Paparchantis
Cover Designer:	Michael Dubowe
Production Artist:	Michelle Lee

Contents

Acknowledgments

I wrote my first grant nearly 14 years ago when I was asked to create a parent and community volunteers partnership project as part of my administrative internship. Once I was given the assignment, I felt overwhelmed on how to identify prospective funders for the project and how to develop a grant proposal. I immediately contacted my administrative internship adviser, who provided me with a self-published manuscript on how to identify funders and write an educational grant proposal. Through her guidance and mentorship, I completed my first grant after several rewrites. The grant received favorable responses from two prospective funders!

Since that initial experience, I have assisted hundreds of educators and human service agency providers in developing strategic fundraising plans to support their long-term program development goals. Through these strategic planning sessions, I have learned how to create grant templates that assist program developers in constructing clearly defined grant plans according to a funder's requirements. The work is challenging and exhilarating as educators and community-based organizations share their resources to (1) define who they are, (2) identify the types of services that they can collaboratively provide, and (3) collectively create new programs to better serve their students' needs. When diverse stakeholders collaborate for streamlined service delivery, funding options for a collaborative project can significantly increase.

The grant development process described in this book has evolved over the past 14 years through diverse field experiences with urban and suburban schools, school districts, community-based organizations, government agencies, and partnerships with foundations and businesses. I am indebted to Dr. Lee Mahon, who served as my first grant development mentor and provided me with the encouragement to become a successful grantwriter. Special thanks go to Dr. Mitsu Kumagai, who has assisted me in developing diverse community collaborations that respond to emerging needs. Carl Liljenstolpe helped design and pilot a donor development computer database system to support diverse fund development marketing needs. Zuraida Peres and the Portuguese Organization for Social Services' staff helped me field test innovative partnership development strategies to access diversified funding sources.

As Director of the University of Southern California Rossier School of Education Center for Research in Education Finance (CREF), Dr. Lawrence (Larry) O. Picus sponsors all of my field research and publications. I want to thank Larry's wife, Susan, and his engaging 7-year-old son, Matthew, for allowing me to occasionally collaborate with Larry on weekends to meet manuscript deadlines.

Dr. Reynaldo Baca from the Center for Multilingual, Multicultural Research in the Rossier School of Education at the University of Southern California continues to serve as my social conscience in developing equitable school programs for culturally diverse populations. Professor William B. Michael from the Division of Educational Psychology and Technology in the Rossier School of Education at the University of Southern California has helped me create alternative assessment instruments for measuring the impact of these partnership programs on students' academic performance. Professor Stuart Gothold from the Rossier School of Education at the University of Southern California continues to provide transformational leadership support in forming new school and community collaborative partnerships.

Appreciation goes to Dr. Magaly Lavadenz from Loyola Marymount University, the Rossier School of Education's former Dean, Guilbert C. Hentschke, and the Rossier School of Education's former Professional Studies Manager, Jeffrey Davis, for sponsoring and coordinating the continuing education program component.

I would not have been able to complete the ongoing research for this project without the commitment and sponsorship from the Compton Unified School District. Special thanks go to former Accountability Officer Cathy Jones, Compliance Administrator Tom Brown, and former State Administrator Dr. Randolph Ward who have supported my efforts in creating and piloting unique and streamlined grant development and implementation strategies.

Jacques Bordeaux, a former employee of the California State University, Los Angeles, ACCESS Center, provided me with a vision of how urban students and their families can partner with teachers and businesses to prepare students for acceptance into competitive higher educational institutions and for careers in science and math. Special thanks go to Yvette King-Berg from Project GRAD Los Angeles, Karen Matsui from the Achievement Council, and Cambria Smith from the Volunteer Center of Los Angeles, who have provided me with countless hours of guidance on how to create innovative programs that streamline service delivery systems for underachieving youth.

Three publications have been instrumental in the preparation of this book. Soraya M. Coley's and Cynthia A. Scheinberg's *Proposal Writing*, published by Sage Publications in 2000, provided me with a simplified blueprint on the various topics that should be considered in the grant development process with suggestions on how to streamline the process. The *Grantwriter's Internet Companion* is an excellent resource book written by Susan Peterson, published by Corwin Press in 2001. This reference book can help program developers use computerized research strategies to locate various types of funders through the Internet. Henry Levin's and Patrick McEwan's *Cost-Effectiveness Analysis: Methods and Applications*, published by Sage in 2001, provided me with a firm foundation on fiscally astute budget considerations and how to fiscally manage diversified funding resources.

Finally, heartfelt thanks go to my family who has made countless sacrifices for me to pursue my passionate dream of developing innovative grants that support the academic achievement of culturally and economically diverse students.

About the Author

Mary Ann Burke, Ed.D., is Adjunct Lecturer for the College of Education Department of Educational Administration and Policy Studies at California State University, Sacramento. Dr. Burke is also Adjunct Assistant Professor in the Rossier School of Education at the University of Southern California, specializing in resource development for education. She has provided administrative program development, grantwriting assistance, and assessment support to various Los Angeles County urban school districts, charter schools, and community-based organizations. During the past 3 years, she has assisted various school districts and community agencies in securing more than 100 million dollars in educational and social service grant funding. She is the former director of the Community Partnership Coalition VISTA Project, sponsored by Fenton Avenue Charter School. The project recruits and trains parents and community volunteers to serve as mentors and tutors in the classroom. She is the coauthor of *Recruiting Volunteers, Creative Fundraising,* and *Developing Community-Empowered Schools.*

Introduction

Teachers and administrators typically feel overwhelmed when a grant application must be completed. Traditionally, these practitioners have limited experience developing savvy fund development plans and writing well-constructed, articulate grants for funding. When grant requests are distributed to busy school administrators and teachers, few have the knowledge required to

- Create a simplified process for managing all grantwriting activities with diverse stakeholders
- Identify an effective marketing strategy to fund an effective educational program
- Consider various options for collaborating with diverse stakeholders
- Effectively organize and time manage the grant development process
- Understand the integral components of defining a grant proposal's need, program design, and measurable evaluation plan
- Design a clearly articulated grant proposal template that addresses all of the funder's requirements
- Modify program proposals that meet diverse funder needs and respond to diverse community needs
- Establish a program sustainability plan that ensures unlimited funding and community support

■ THE VALUE OF EFFECTIVE GRANTWRITING

This book is dedicated to providing school districts and site staff with effective strategies for writing program grants that will leverage resources for diverse stakeholder groups. Effective grantwriting for program development can contribute to a school's overall economic growth and to the school community's sustainability. This topic is vital for educators because grantwriting is becoming far more complex for educational practitioners. More school sites must link community-based health and human care services to expanded family education services to better meet the needs of their students' families. Additionally, more school site programs are required to demonstrate outcome-based evaluations to sustain funding and to leverage additional funding from diverse stakeholders.

The grantwriting process described in this book has been field tested for over a decade. It is based on survival grantwriting strategies used in Los Angeles County urban schools, a rural San Diego County charter school, and in northern Californian suburban communities. The survival strategies support educational grantwriting methods books and the overall grantwriting strategies promoted by national foundation fundraising associations. By merging the methods training provided for educational grantwriting with the best practices provided by national foundation fundraising associations, this book can create a new level of understanding for all educational practitioners in effective grant development with diverse stakeholder groups.

■ ORGANIZATION OF THIS BOOK

The book's eight chapters focus on the best practices that have helped educational practitioners and diverse stakeholders write successful funding proposals. This book will help them organize their grantwriting activities to develop clearly articulated grant proposals. By merging the school-community relations training currently provided in teacher education courses with the resource development strategies identified by educational economists and grantwriters, educational practitioners and stakeholders can create grant proposals that can raise the achievement level and career aspirations of underserved students. The following chapter descriptions summarize a simplified process for completing educational grant applications that have a high probability of being funded.

Chapter 1 describes effective practices and a process for grant development and implementation that helps diverse stakeholder groups easily create clearly articulated grant proposals within a limited amount of time.

Chapter 2 highlights how to (1) define key identifier needs within a specific program that a funder may wish to support, (2) create a matrix of prospective funders for various program components, and (3) customize the marketing of an educational program to meet the funding interests of specific funders.

Chapter 3 defines activities that ensure that all stakeholders can provide program support for the critical program delivery of services.

Chapter 4 provides school practitioners with effective strategies for creating a grant in a responsive and timely manner, including reviewing grant specifications, scheduling grant informational and needs assessment meetings, creating and completing grant templates with appropriate stakeholders, and convening follow-up meetings with appropriate stakeholders.

Chapter 5 describes the various grant proposal components found in federal grants, state grants, local grants, and foundation grants.

Chapter 6 illustrates how grantwriters formulate grant templates that respond to the unique funding specifications and requirements of funders and highlights an effective grant template completion process.

Chapter 7 examines various strategies a school or district can use to identifying other funders, community resources, service delivery partners, and cross-selling strategies that can provide additional program support.

Chapter 8 provides a long-range fundraising plan worksheet to assist educational practitioners in strategically evaluating all current programs being funded by diverse funders and identifying any overlaps in service delivery or need for added services. Through this strategic planning tool, schools and school districts can effectively plan for future program and funding needs.

1

A Simplified Process
for Grant Development
and Implementation

A simplified grant development process requires (1) a strategic prioritization of program services a school or organization intends to accomplish within the next year and within the next 3 to 5 years, (2) the identification of an appropriate fund development plan that will support short- and long-term program development goals, and (3) an effective grant development process for submitting, tracking, and implementing grants. Although the grant development process may appear logical and easy to execute, many novice grantwriters become overwhelmed with how to integrate and time manage grant development responsibilities into their daily schedules. This chapter will describe an effective sequence of events that can ensure successful grant development and project implementation for large grants that may incorporate subcontracting to other agencies and that are likely to be renewed and amplified.

STRATEGIC PLANNING
FOR PROGRAM DEVELOPMENT ∎

Effective fund development requires the prioritization of various program activities. Typically, when a school leadership team is asked to identify what it plans to accomplish within a particular program, various team members have very different perceptions about what specific services or strategies should occur first to better serve their students' needs. For example, when trying to define which program components may best help students increase their academic performance in language arts, leadership team members might suggest a combination of the following solutions:

- Staff development training for teachers on the core curriculum, on how the curriculum aligns to the state's content standards, and on various effective instructional strategies for teachers to use with diverse student groups
- Classroom coaching support on classroom organization and daily activities to support student productivity
- Staff development on differentiated instructional delivery models
- Staff coaching on how to integrate project based learning into the curriculum
- Safety net tutorial programs to assist students displaying difficulty in learning
- Test-taking strategies and stress reduction training
- Parent and community volunteer programs that support student achievement
- School site health and human care programs for students
- Parent education programs that provide child development and academic support training
- Community partnerships with businesses that provide career mentorship activities

When leadership team members cannot agree on what activities are the most critical for immediate development, it is vital for the group to take the time to create both short- and long-term strategic plans. Once a leadership team has clarified what specific activities it plans to accomplish during the current and future school years, it will be prepared to identify appropriate funders to support specific program needs. Form 1.1 is a sample strategic planning form that can be used by the leadership team for assessing and prioritizing various programs for short- and long-term expansion. Form 1.2 provides a sample resource development workplan that can assist the leadership team in identifying program funding options and strategies for obtaining funding.

■ HOW TO FIND FUNDERS

Funding options can initially be identified through Internet searches on federal, state, county, and local funders and on community and

(text continues on p. 8)

Form 1.1. Sample Strategic Planning Instrument for Prioritizing and Assessing Your School's Program Component Needs

Consider the following program components at your school and circle the appropriate numerical value (1 = high and 5 = low) to rate the priority for developing this program component:

	High				**Low**
1. The academic program content	1	2	3	4	5
2. Academic textbooks and instructional materials	1	2	3	4	5
3. Teacher training on integrating standards into course content	1	2	3	4	5
4. Teacher training on differentiated instructional strategies	1	2	3	4	5
5. Teacher training on project-based learning	1	2	3	4	5
6. Teacher training on parent and community volunteer programs	1	2	3	4	5
7. Teacher training on classroom organization and management	1	2	3	4	5
8. Teacher training on student portfolios and authentic assessments	1	2	3	4	5
9. Teacher training on adapting curriculum to respond to students' needs	1	2	3	4	5
10. Teacher training on_____	1	2	3	4	5
11. Tutorial support services for students	1	2	3	4	5
12. Stress reduction and test-taking strategy training for students	1	2	3	4	5
13. Health and human care support services for students	1	2	3	4	5
14. Parent education on child rearing and academic support strategies	1	2	3	4	5
15. Mentorship career development programs with businesses	1	2	3	4	5
16. Family literacy training and family academic enrichment activities	1	2	3	4	5
17. Visual and performing arts programs	1	2	3	4	5
18. Science and math enrichment activities	1	2	3	4	5
19. After-school childcare and academic support programs	1	2	3	4	5
20. School site student and family recreational programs	1	2	3	4	5

(Continued)

Form 1.1. (Continued)

	High				Low
21. Computer literacy training for students and parents	1	2	3	4	5
22. English-as-a-second-language training for families	1	2	3	4	5
23. After-school organized sports programs for students	1	2	3	4	5
24. Student and family school-sponsored service learning projects	1	2	3	4	5
25. Gang prevention and conflict resolution training	1	2	3	4	5
26. Drug and alcohol prevention programs	1	2	3	4	5
27. Counseling support services for students and their families	1	2	3	4	5
28. School and community safety training programs	1	2	3	4	5
29. Community problem-solving meetings sponsored by the school	1	2	3	4	5
30. Other program development _____	1	2	3	4	5

List the three highest rated needs identified in the survey:

1. _____

2. _____

3. _____

List three strategies or programs that would support these prioritized needs:

1. _____

2. _____

3. _____

Form 1.2. Sample Program and Resource Development Workplan

List a specific program need: _____

In the chart below, list the school's current program components or activities.
Identify current funding sources or community partners for each program component.

Program Component or Activity	*Funding Sources and Community Partners*

(Continued)

Form 1.2. (Continued)

Based on the information provided on your chart, list 10 steps that your school can pursue to fund and provide all identified priority program components or activities:

1. _____

2. _____

3. _____

4. _____

5. _____

6. _____

7. _____

8. _____

9. _____

10. _____

(Continued)

Form 1.2. Continued)

In the chart below, list five stakeholder groups, government agencies, community and corporate foundations, businesses, and community agencies that can provide or support various program activities. Describe the services and resources each identified stakeholder group can contribute to a program component.

Name of Stakeholder Group	*Description of Service or Resource*
1.	
2.	
3.	
4.	
5.	

corporate foundations. Web sites that provide comprehensive funding searches include Fundsnet Services Online, The Internet Prospector, Grantmaker Information, and Council on Foundations. Significant funder Web site addresses or links to various funders are provided in Table 1.1.

Community foundations and nonprofit funding resource centers provide fundraising training, funding informational directories, libraries, and grantwriter referrals. The Foundation Center in New York publishes fundraising directories and general grantwriting books. Fundraising periodicals include the *Chronicle of Philanthropy, Nonprofit Times, CD Publications, Philanthropy Today,* and *Nonprofit World Magazine.* In addition, the U.S. Department of Education and state departments of education publish numerous articles and studies on educational grantwriting and program development.

ATTENDING FUNDER
INFORMATIONAL MEETINGS

All prospective funders should be contacted and asked to send their grant development guidelines, a description of their funded projects, foundation annual reports, and information about a bidder's conference or request for proposal meetings. Funding guidelines will include specific limitations on the types of programs that are funded, preferred geographical locations for programs, and specific deadlines to submit various documents. It is critical to understand each funder's grant development policies, procedures, and protocol requirements to support a successful grant development process. The grant development team should attend all funder grant meetings to learn more about a grant's requirements. Topics typically discussed at these informational sessions include

- A review of the request for proposal announcement and application packet
- Background information about legislation supporting the grant's development
- Demographic and statistical data supporting the need for the request for proposal
- Relevant research and resources available for grant development and implementation
- A review of proven research models that support the grant's development
- A grant development timeline of activities to support effective grant completion
- Strategies and resources for collaborating with government and community agencies

(text continues on p. 12)

Table 1.1 Funder Web Site Addresses

Funder	Web Site Address
United States Department of Education, with links to discretionary grant program offices and initiatives	www.ed.gov
The Foundation Center, with links to 1,000 Web sites	www.foundationcenter.org
The Ford Foundation	www.fordfound.org
The David and Lucile Packard Foundation	www.packfound.org
W. K. Kellogg Foundation	www.wkkf.org
Bank of America Foundation	www.bankofamerica.com/foundation
The American Association of School Administrators, with links to funding	www.aasa.org/issues_and_insights/funding/index.htm
Local source teacher grants	www.teachergrants.org
eSchool News School Funding Center	www.eschoolnews.org/funding
School Grants	www.schoolgrants.org
International Reading Association	www.reading.org
National Art Education Foundation	www.naea-reston.org/programs.html

Form 1.3. Sample Prospective Funder Evaluation

List a specific program need or program component: _____

Based on your research on prospective funders, complete the chart below to evaluate the feasibility of receiving program funding and additional grant development information.

Funder's Name	Funding Limitations and Informational Meeting Agenda of Topics and Date	Types of Funder Documents Received (RFPs, Annual Reports, etc.)

(Continued)

Form 1.3. (Continued)

After attending each grant informational meeting and/or reviewing all funder documents, list those funders who you will send grant proposals to and note their deadlines:

Funder Contact's Name, Address, Phone Number, and E-mail Address	Letter of Intent Deadline	Grant Proposal Deadline

- Program evaluations models to measure the grant's goals, objectives, and activities within a specific timeline
- Strategies and models for successfully writing competitive grants
- A rubric of how the grant will be evaluated for funding
- Grant application forms to be completed with instructions
- The grant budget form to be completed with a sample budget and instructions
- Strategies for creating diversified funding and sustaining the program
- Any attachments and supporting documents required

Form 1.3 provides a Sample Prospective Funder Evaluation that can help school grant development teams evaluate the feasibility of receiving funding from prospective funders.

■ DESIGNING RESPONSIVE GRANT TEMPLATES

Once a school's grant development team identifies an appropriate project funder, it is critical to summarize all information that the grant proposal requests by creating a grant template. A grant template can help a grantwriter organize and answer the information requested by a funder's proposal specifications. It can include an outline of the proposal's informational requirements with supporting tables that summarize critical data requested by the funder. Most grant proposals request the following information:

- A grant proposal introduction
- A description of the school's demographics and needs
- The proposed program with goals, objectives, timeline, and activities to respond to a need
- The staffing qualifications and school's capacity to support the proposed program
- An evaluation plan
- A program budget and budget narrative
- The program's plan for sustainability beyond the grant funding cycle

A grant template with supporting tables can be constructed to respond to each of the grant proposal's sections. For example, a grant table can be constructed to summarize the program's need with a list of specific community demographics and school data that justify the problem and need for the program. In addition to a table that summarizes the need, the template can include an introduction to the need section and a section for proposing a program that can respond to the need. Grant templates can help the grantwriter in the following ways:

- Organize his or her thoughts in response to a specific funder's requirements
- Facilitate grant development sessions with diverse stakeholders
- Assign various sections of the grant template to diverse stakeholders for input
- Maintain focus in answering the questions and collecting the data requested by the funder
- Consolidate and edit stakeholders' responses into a cohesive and well-researched grant proposal

Chapter 5 will describe how to respond to these various grant proposal components and Chapter 6 will describe how to design a responsive grant template that can sufficiently answer all grant proposal questions.

CREATING DIVERSIFIED GRANT DEVELOPMENT TEAMS ■

Although school leadership teams initially determine what specific programs must be expanded or developed to meet the unique learning needs of their students, most funders require a collaborative problem-solving process for grant development and implementation. Key grant stakeholders include (1) those who have a concern about the outcome of an intervention, (2) those who occupy key positions of authority who can act upon the implementation of the intervention, and (3) those who can facilitate the implementation of recommendations. Within a school community, key stakeholders can include

- Students
- Teachers
- School site and central office administrators
- Program support and clerical staff
- Parents and community members
- Community-based organizations
- Local businesses
- Legislators
- Higher educational and research institutions
- Government agencies and nonprofit organizations
- Funders
- Unlikely allies

Chapter 3 discusses how various stakeholder groups can collaborate to provide the school with critical and supplemental services within the grant proposal. A school's grant development team can include key stakeholder groups in formulating (1) a grant proposal's needs assessment; (2) the program plan with measurable goals, objectives, activities, and timelines; and (3) the program component evaluation strategies. The grant development team should also identify any other stakeholders who can provide program development information, technical assistance, program implementation services, or evaluation support.

MODIFYING GRANT PROPOSALS TO MEET DIVERSE FUNDERS' NEEDS

Once a grant program plan has been created to meet a funder's unique grant proposal specifications, all grant proposal components can be modified to respond to other diverse funder requirements for sustained program support. Chapter 7 explores how diverse stakeholders can repackage a grant to submit it to untraditional educational partners. Typically, many health and human care subcontractors receive part of their program funding from community foundations. When a health and human care agency subcontracts to provide services at a school site, the program is indirectly funded by the foundations that provide funding to the health and human care agency. This collaboration can leverage added funding for new programs at the school site and sustain additional program support. Effective collaborative partners can help in the following ways:

- Streamline and improve a school's delivery of diverse educational services
- Facilitate a school community's problem-solving process for new program development
- Leverage new or expanded resources and revenues for the school
- Enhance the school's public relations image within the community

In essence, collaborative schools can become the hub of their community's educational growth and economic survival. To support this infusion of community resources, the collaborative school must create a governance structure, policies, and procedures that enhance and nurture the growth of these partnerships.

2

Marketing Strategies for Educational Program Funding

A n educational program can be developed and promoted to various funders for diversified funding and program sustainability. Once a school or school district identifies the specific needs and programs it wishes to develop for funding, the program can be packaged to meet a specific funder's interests and requirements. The following strategies can help a school leverage diversified funding to meet a specific program need:

- Identifying various needs within a program that a funder may wish to support
- Creating a matrix of prospective funders that can help define various program components
- Customizing the marketing of a program to meet the interests of specific funders

When reviewing the funding interests of different funders, it is critical for the school's grant development team to be able to separate various program activities to leverage diverse funding sources. Table 2.1 illustrates how various activities in an after-school program can be separately described to meet diversified funder needs. Table 2.2 illustrates how various activities described in Table 2.1 can receive support from a matrix of different funders. Using Tables 2.1 and 2.2 as an example of how to define various activities in a program and create a matrix of prospective funders, create your own activity description form using Form 2.1 and your own matrix of funders using Form 2.2.

CUSTOMIZING THE ■ MARKETING OF A PROGRAM

Each funder has specific funding interests. How a school describes and markets its programs to a specific funder will affect (1) whether the school will be funded for a specific program, (2) how much the school can request for a specific program, and (3) how the school can access additional funding by modifying a program description. For example, consider an after-school program for students that provides childcare, tutorial and academic enrichment activities, conflict resolution, and organized sports. The school is located in a community with a high incidence of poverty, gang-related crime, and low academic performance. When considering funders, the school might initially apply for program funding only for childcare, academic tutoring, recreational and sports programs, and counseling support services. However, by further developing various program components to meet the safety, counseling, academic, and career development needs of the multistressed students, additional funding sources could provide the following:

- School safety funding for providing students with a safe and drug-free after-school program that provides substance abuse and crime prevention education

- Counseling support funding that provides individual and small-group counseling to students regarding substance abuse, gang-related behavior, conflict resolution, how to build healthy relationships, career exploration, and planning for higher education

- Reading and math improvement funding to hire and train tutors and extra-duty certificated teachers from the school site

- Mentorship funding that includes training the school's volunteers to support students in their career development and that provides students with business internships

- Computer literacy and technology training to support students' academic improvement and career development

- Parent education funding on child development and academic support strategies

Added funding can also be requested when considering the formal and informal components of each program. For example, if the school provides childcare to students, added funding can be provided to train college students studying child development to work with multi-stressed

(text continues on p. 20)

Table 2.1 Sample After-School Program Describing Various Activities

Program Activity or Funding Interest	Description of Activity
Childcare	The school site after-school program provides childcare to elementary school age students from 3 p.m. until 5 p.m., Mondays through Fridays.
Nutritional snack	Students will be provided with a nutritional snack at 3:30 p.m. each day.
Tutorial and academic enrichment activities	Students will be provided with one-on-one tutorial support 30 minutes twice a week to improve reading skills and reinforce the grade level Open Court curriculum.
Organized sports	Students will participate in an organized sports team 2 afternoons a week.
Conflict resolution and counseling support	Students will participate in a conflict resolution group activity meeting 1 hour per week and receive training on effective conflict resolution strategies from the school's counselors.
Computer literacy and technology training	Students will be provided with computer literacy instruction twice a week for 30 minutes.
Visual and performing arts	Students will receive performing arts instruction in art, drama, music, or theater 1 hour per week.
Science and math	Students will receive science and math tutorial support 30 minutes twice a week and participate in a group science and math activity once a week.

Table 2.2 Sample After-School Program Matrix of Diversified Funding Sources

Program Activity or Funding Interest	Matrix of Diversified Funding Sources
Childcare	Welfare-to-Work federal and state funding 21st Century Learning Center funding
Nutritional snack	Subcontract with the district's food services program with leveraging of federal and state funding
Tutorial and academic enrichment activities	Reading Excellence Act federal and state funding AmeriCorps federal funding Mentorship Initiative state and private foundation funding
Organized sports	21st Century Learning Center funding After-school safe schools state funding Community police activity league volunteers
Conflict resolution and counseling support	After-school safe schools state funding Health and human care community agency subcontractors
Computer literacy and technology training	College science and math academic preparation program Engineering community mentorship program Federal, state, and private foundation funders
Visual and performing arts	Community performing arts subcontractors Local colleges and university performing arts departments Museum docent program and foundation funders
Science and math	College science and math academic preparation program Engineering community mentorship program

Form 2.1. Sample Form Describing Various Activities for the _____ Program

Program Activity or Funding Interest	Description of Activity

students. In addition, marriage and family counseling interns can be paid stipends for providing students and their families counseling support and parent education services. Academic support and mentorship services can also be expanded to include all students registered in the after-school program when considering the informal role modeling and academic student support services being provided in all program components. Finally, counseling funding can be expanded to include the sports activities when considering students are taught how to work together as a team and reduce group conflict.

To sustain and expand any school program, it is vital for schools to recognize the interrelations of various program components and market these interrelated components to funders. Table 2.3 demonstrates how an after-school childcare program expanded its services to students by identifying its interrelated program components and the various informal activities within each program. Create your own interrelated program chart using Form 2.3.

Form 2.2. Sample Matrix of Diversified Funding Sources for the _____ Program

Program Activity or Funding Interest	Matrix of Diversified Funding Sources

Table 2.3 Sample After-School Program Matrix of Expanded Services

Program Activity or Funding Interest	Interrelated Program Components and Informal Activities
Childcare	• Safe and drug-free program environment • Emergency preparation and home safety training • Substance abuse prevention education • Building safe neighborhoods and crime prevention • Babysitting certificate programs for students • Career training and college internships for students majoring in child development, teacher preparation, and counseling
Nutritional snack	• Nutritional science units of study • Cooking recipe math units • Safe food preparation • Recreational cooking classes • Career mentorship and internship experiences in food services and nutritional sciences
Tutorial and academic enrichment activities	• Reading and math improvement tutoring by volunteer mentors and extra-duty certificated teachers from the school • Business internships that reinforce reading, language arts, math, social studies, and science academic skills • Building academic skills through visual and performing arts • Study skill and test-taking strategy training
Organized sports	• Conflict resolution • How to build healthy team relationships • Crime prevention and gang-related behavior education

Table 2.3 (Continued)

Program Activity or Funding Interest	Interrelated Program Components and Informal Activities
Conflict resolution and counseling support	• Conflict resolution and how to build healthy relationships • Substance abuse prevention education • Crime prevention and gang-related behavior education • Career exploration and planning for higher education • Parent education on child development and academic support strategies • Career training and college internships for students majoring in child development, teacher preparation, and counseling
Computer literacy and technology training	• Building academic skills through technology training • Business internships • Service learning community-based projects that emphasize computer literacy and technology skill development
Visual and performing arts	• Building academic skills through visual and performing arts • Business internships • Service learning community-based projects that emphasize visual and performing arts skill development
Science and math	• Reading and math improvement tutoring by volunteer mentors and extra-duty certificated teachers from the school • Business internships

Form 2.3. Sample Matrix of Expanded Services for the _____ Program

Program Activity or Funding Interest	Interrelated Program Components and Informal Activities

3

Integrated
Program
Collaborations

Identifying diverse stakeholders beyond the traditional educational partners requires creativity, networking, and strategic planning to provide continued and sustained support for educational program implementation. The following activities ensure that all stakeholders who can provide program support are identified and included in the critical program delivery of services:

- Identify community stakeholders who can collaborate and provide critical and supplemental program services.

- Build collaborative partnerships with key stakeholders who have influence in leveraging program resources in a particular program area.

- Brainstorm with key stakeholders in creating supplemental program services to enhance a program's delivery of services.

The following sections will describe a process for identifying prospective community partners who can serve as subcontractors in providing specific contractual services in various programs and who can leverage additional funding that may not be accessible to schools.

IDENTIFYING COLLABORATIVE COMMUNITY ■ PARTNERS FOR CRITICAL SERVICES

Once a school determines the programs it will expand to meet the critical needs of its students, all the school's stakeholders must be surveyed to determine what public sector organizations, community agencies, and local businesses can provide various program components. Form 3.1 provides a sample survey that can be distributed to various stakeholders for identifying organizations and businesses that can provide specific services to support a school's programs. Table 3.1 provides a sample of identified public sector organizations, community agencies, and local businesses that may be used for a school's after-school childcare program. Many of the public sector and community-based organizations listed in Table 3.1 may receive funding for their program services from the federal government, state government, local funders, private foundations, and private sponsors. For example, a community career counseling and mentoring organization that receives foundation funding may not have access to students at their school sites. When considering this example, remember that a school's core business is education and the community agency's core business is providing emotional and career development counseling and mentoring services. In reviewing the funding preferences of private and public foundations, most funders limit direct access of funds designated for counseling and mentoring services to only health and human care nonprofit service providers. Many of these funders would, however, encourage a community career counseling and mentoring organization to provide direct services to students at their school sites.

Considering the sample information provided in Table 3.1, Forms 3.1 and 3.2 are for a school to use in identifying its own community partners for providing a specific program service. Community partners can collaborate in a program's service delivery by

- Bringing existing services to the school site
- Helping a school or school district identify effective strategies for program delivery
- Expanding or modifying existing services to better meet the needs of the school community
- Providing services at locations and times that are more accessible to the families who will be served
- Networking with other service providers and the school or school district to streamline the delivery of services and eliminate duplication of services
- Supporting the school or school district in accessing funding and services from funders who traditionally do not provide direct funding to schools

(text continues on p. 31)

Table 3.1 Sample of Identified Community Partners to Support an After-School Program

Program Activity or Funding Interest	Identified Community Partners
Childcare	• Childcare program managed by a private business • The American Red Cross to provide emergency preparation and home safety training • A counseling agency to provide substance abuse prevention education • The local law enforcement agency to help create a neighborhood watch program for safe neighborhoods and crime prevention • Babysitting certificate programs for students offered through the adult and community education program • Career training and college internships for students majoring in child development, teacher preparation, and counseling offered through community and state colleges
Nutritional snack	• Nutritional science units of study provided by a hospital • Cooking recipe math units provided by a university college readiness program • Safe food preparation and cooking classes provided by a community college health services certificate program • Career internships provided by restaurants
Tutorial and academic enrichment activities	• Reading and math improvement tutoring by an AmeriCorps service learning project sponsored by a local college • Tutorial services provided by a private business • Business internships provided by local industry partners that reinforce academic skills • Study skill and test-taking strategy training provided by private sector test preparation businesses
Organized sports	• Conflict resolution provided by a counseling agency • How to build healthy team relationships provided by local sports team volunteers • Crime prevention and gang-related behavior education provided by a local law enforcement agency

(Continued)

Table 3.1 (Continued)

Program Activity or Funding Interest	Identified Community Partners
Conflict resolution and counseling support	• Conflict resolution and how to build healthy relationships by a college counseling intern program • Substance abuse prevention education provided by a local substance recovery program volunteer • Crime prevention and gang-related behavior education provided by a community watch neighborhood group of trained citizens • Career exploration and planning for higher education provided by industry mentor volunteers • Parent education provided by the adult and community education program and college interns
Computer literacy and technology training	• Building academic skills through technology training by industry volunteers • Business internships though local industry partners • AmeriCorps service learning community-based projects that emphasize computer literacy and technology skill development sponsored by colleges
Visual and performing arts	• Building academic skills through visual and performing arts community agencies and museum docent programs • Business internships through local businesses • Community agency service learning projects that emphasize visual and performing arts skill development
Science and math	• Reading and math improvement tutoring by AmeriCorps volunteers sponsored by a local college • Business internships through industry partners

Form 3.1. Sample Survey to Identify Community Partners for the _____ Program

Program Activity or Funding Interest	*Data Profile and Service Description of Prospective Community Partner*
	Name of organization: Address: Phone number: Description and fees for service: Service capability and staffing: Current service location:
	Name of organization: Address: Phone number: Description and fees for service: Service capability and staffing: Current service location:

Form 3.2. Sample Identified Community Partner Table for the _____ Program

Program Activity	Identified Community Partners

BUILDING COLLABORATIVE PARTNERSHIPS FOR LEVERAGING PROGRAM RESOURCES ■

Once a school's stakeholders identify a variety of community and business partners that can provide different program components and leverage resources, it is critical to invite all stakeholders to an informational program meeting at the school site. At the meeting, the school can provide a summary or overview of the following:

- All current programs the school is developing or expanding

- The school's current capacity and staffing to support all current and emerging programs

- A strategic plan with a schedule and timeline of specific activities each program will implement to support expansion and development

- Current community partners and funding sources to support each program's development

- A proposed description or strategy of how each community partner can support specific program components

- The proposed benefits of becoming a collaborative partner in the program, including the increase of services that a partner can provide in the program, the potential for increased funding, increased visibility in the community and among key funders, and the value and stability of working with an established school or school district

After providing this background information, each community partner should prepare a proposal to the school on the following key concepts:

- A description of the services the agency currently provides

- A summary of the organization's background, capacity, and current staffing to support various programs

- A proposed program overview of how the organization can support each of the school's program development or expansion areas

- A budget summarizing how much it will cost to provide various services

- An accounting of the existing funding sources and funding amounts the organization can use to support the various school programs

- A fundraising plan on how the organization will leverage funding to meet the needs of the school

- An evaluation plan of how the organization will determine the outcome of its program and the program's impact on student achievement and behavior

- A listing of any other program collaborators who must be recruited to support the organization's service delivery

- A cost-benefit analysis of why it would be favorable for the organization to provide direct services to the students as a subcontractor to the school rather than have the school create the infrastructure and management for the program

After each prospective community partner provides an extensive analysis and plan for service delivery, the school's staff can evaluate the feasibility of using each community partner within the school's current organizational and financial structure. Typically, this comprehensive analysis will clearly indicate which community partners would best meet the needs of a school community's diverse population. Furthermore, a cost-benefit analysis may indicate that it will be much cheaper for a school district to subcontract childcare or tutoring services instead of creating its own infrastructure to manage and develop the program. Form 3.3 provides a sample template for assisting a prospective community partner in creating a plan for providing school site services. Form 3.4 provides a sample budget analysis template for a prospective community partner.

BRAINSTORMING WITH KEY STAKEHOLDERS FOR CREATING SUPPLEMENTAL PROGRAM SERVICES

Once the school invites prospective community partners to the school site to formulate their program expansion or enhancement service plans, other community groups may be identified for streamlined service delivery. For example, an after-school childcare program can further expand services to include

- Medical examinations and immunizations provided by mobile community health clinics

- Individual mental health counseling services provided by mobile mental health clinics

- Hobby and social club activities sponsored by youth development community agencies

- Field trip excursions provided by museums and other community agencies

- Parent education seminars from parent education consultants

- Tutorial support provided by private tutoring businesses

- Performing arts activities provided by local artists

Form 3.3. Sample Community Partner Plan for Providing School Site Services for the _____ Program

Program Activity	*Organization's Service Delivery Plan*
	Description of current program services: Background, capacity, and current program staffing: School site plan to program development/expansion: Program goals, objectives, timeline, assigned staffing: Program evaluation plan with timeline:
	Description of current program services: Background, capacity, and current program staffing: School site plan to program development/expansion: Program goals, objectives, timeline, assigned staffing: Program evaluation plan with timeline:

Form 3.4. Sample Budget Analysis for Prospective Community Partner

Simplified Program Budget	Proposed Expenditures	Other Funding Sources and Amounts
Certificated salaries Classified salaries Employee benefits Books and supplies Travel Utilities (not communication) Building and room rentals Printing and copying Professional consulting services Phones and postage Equipment Other: Total proposed expenditures		
Fundraising Plan for Securing Added Funding	Future or Expanded Funding Expenditures	Proposed Matched Funding Sources and Amounts
Certificated salaries Classified salaries Employee benefits Books and supplies Travel Utilities (not communication) Building and room rentals Printing and copying Professional consulting services Phones and postage Equipment Other: Future proposed expenditures		

- Counseling services provided by community counseling agencies
- Case management services provided by social service agencies
- Immunization and legal support services for families provided by community legal support agencies and governmental agencies
- Basic needs services provided by emergency assistance agencies
- Family reading programs provided by the local library and mobile library programs
- Science and animal visitations provided by local zoos and youth science institutes
- Language arts programs provided by local newspapers and publishers
- Computer literacy programs provided by private computer companies

There are many strategies for further defining primary and supplementary services for program development and expansion. A program stakeholder meeting can help a school further identify and define various stakeholder and subcontractor roles. A subcontractor relationship between the school or school district and a business or agency is formulated when the business or agency agrees to provide the school or school district with specific services described in a contract or a memorandum of understanding. Examples of subcontractor partnerships can include (1) a childcare agency that will provide the management of an after-school program on the school site, (2) a community sports association that will provide a year-round sports program for the students attending the childcare program, and (3) a tutoring assistance business that will create a family literacy program component through the after-school childcare program. Table 3.2 provides a sample agenda for facilitating a program development planning meeting that can identify prospective subcontractors who can support a school's or school district's program delivery. Boxes 3.1, 3.2, and 3.3 provide examples of how a school can assign subcontractors to various program components and how to create memorandums of understanding on the roles, responsibilities, and problem resolution process of individual subcontractors for donated and purchased services.

Table 3.2 Sample Program Development Planning Agenda

9:00 – 9:30	Introductions and review the agenda
9:30 – 9:45	Review the program goals, objectives, and activities
9:45 – 10:30	Break into small groups to complete the Sample Stakeholder Brainstorming Form for Creating Supplemental Services in Box 3.3
10:30 – 11:00	Each group will summarize the results of their brainstorming session within 5 minutes
11:00 – 11:30	After all groups present their reports, the facilitator will prioritize primary and supplementary services and identify the subcontractor to provide each service by having all participants vote on each service to be provided and determine which subcontractor will provide the service
11:30 – 12:00	Summarize the meeting outcomes and identify next steps

Box 3.1

Sample Stakeholder Brainstorming Form
for Creating Supplemental Services

Review the following case study and then identify all core services your program will provide and any supplemental services you may consider in the future. List specific stakeholder groups that can provide these various services.

Collaboration Example

Achievement Elementary School was awarded a state grant to create a comprehensive after-school program. Primary services would include (1) providing a safe and supportive after-school academic and enrichment program, (2) providing a nutritional snack, and (3) providing recreational and team sports. After meeting with the school's leadership team, parents, students, local community agencies, and businesses, the school decided to formulate the following subcontract partnerships:

1. The Care Childcare Agency would provide the management of the after-school program for students that consisted of academic homework support, arts and crafts, recreational activities, and a daily nutritional snack.

2. The Community Youth Sports Association would organize a year round co-ed team sports program that included soccer, basketball, and baseball.

3. The Tutoring Assistance Company would create a family literacy program and hire extra-duty teachers from the school to staff the program.

4. The Intervention Counseling Agency would provide parent education for parents and self-esteem youth leadership classes for students.

In the table below, identify primary services for your program and all supplementary services. List various community groups and subcontractors that can provide each service.

Primary Services	*Supplementary Services*
Service #1: Subcontractor:	Service #1: Subcontractor:
Service #2: Subcontractor:	Service #2: Subcontractor:
Service #3: Subcontractor:	Service #3: Subcontractor:
Service #4: Subcontractor:	Service #4: Subcontractor:
Service #5: Subcontractor:	Service #5: Subcontractor:

Box 3.2

**Sample Memorandum of
Understanding Describing Subcontractor Services
Provided by a Community Organization to Support a
School Site Childcare Program**

This Memorandum of Understanding confirms that the Care Childcare Agency (the Agency) will be responsible for providing the following services at the Achievement Elementary School (the School). An attached budget itemizes service expenditures that will be billed to the School on a quarterly basis after services have been delivered:

1.   The Agency will provide the management of the after-school program at Achievement Elementary School on Mondays through Fridays from 3:00 p.m. until 6:00 p.m. from September 1, 2002, through June 15, 2003.

2.   The Agency is responsible for hiring, supervising, and managing all program staff and will conduct health and criminal background checks as required by the state laws for childcare providers.

3.   The Agency has all state required licenses and the insurance coverage per the attached documents.

4.   The Agency will provide a safe and supportive after-school academic and enrichment program, a daily nutritional snack, and recreational sports as approved by the school principal on the attached daily program schedule.

5.   The Agency will immediately contact the principal or the principal's designee whenever any student has been injured or an Agency employee has violated any terms of his or her service agreement with the Agency.

6.   The principal or the principal's designee will contact the Agency immediately whenever it is notified of any violation of this service agreement.

Box 3.3

**Sample Memorandum of
Understanding Describing Donated Services
Provided by a Community Organization to
Support a School Site Childcare Program**

This Memorandum of Understanding confirms that the Community Youth Sports Association (the Agency) will be responsible for and donate the following services at the Achievement Elementary School (the School):

1. The Agency will provide the management of the after-school co-ed team sports program for students that includes soccer, basketball, and baseball at Achievement Elementary School on Mondays through Fridays from 3:00 p.m. until 6:00 p.m. from September 1, 2002, through June 15, 2003.

2. The Agency is responsible for hiring, supervising, and managing all program staff and volunteers and will conduct health and criminal background checks as required by the state laws for childcare providers.

3. The Agency has all state required licenses and the insurance coverage per the attached documents.

4. The Agency will provide a safe and supportive team sports program as approved by the school principal on the attached daily program schedule.

5. The Agency will immediately contact the principal or the principal's designee whenever any student has been injured, or an Agency employee or volunteer has violated any terms of his or her service agreement with the Agency.

6. The principal or the principal's designee will contact the Agency immediately whenever it is notified of any violation of this service agreement.

4

Effective Organizational Strategies and Time Management

Most school practitioners have limited grant development time management and organizational skills. This chapter describes how to implement the following effective strategies for creating a grant in a responsive and timely manner:

- Review all grant specification requirements and develop a summary highlighting all grant development requirements and activities within a specified timeline.

- Schedule all funder informational meetings with appropriate leaders.

- Convene a grant needs assessment meeting with all program stakeholders to identify program needs, program plans to respond to those needs, and evaluation instruments that will measure program outcomes.

- Create a worksheet template that all stakeholders can complete for the needs assessment and program development plan.

- Facilitate a meeting with all stakeholders to complete the worksheet template. Work groups and leadership teams can be formed to follow up on all grant development activities.

- Convene follow-up meetings with funders and various stakeholders to complete the grantwriting process and to successfully modify and implement all funded grant plans.

The following sections describe how grant development teams can create effective processes for completing the grant development and implementation cycle.

REVIEWING AND CREATING A
■ SUMMARY OF ALL GRANT REQUIREMENTS

All grants include numerous guidelines for completing the grant development and submission process. Grant announcements typically describe the purpose of funding and applicant specifications. Most grants describe the types of programs that will be considered for funding. Funding priorities are typically given to specific types of community revitalization services provided in a supplemental empowerment zone, an enterprise community designated by the U.S. Department of Housing and Urban Development or the U.S. Department of Agriculture. Other priorities may include (1) services that will be provided in underserved geographical locations or to underserved client groups, (2) specific services that will meet community needs, (3) the formation of specific collaborations to reduce duplicated and fragmented delivery of services, and (4) services that streamline the service delivery process for underserved groups. Grantwriting specifications can include variations of the following:

- Application regulations
- Selection criteria
- Funder's informational meeting and grant training workshops
- Application format requirements including type and size of font, margins, and spacing for text and tables
- Page limits for narratives
- Fiscal agent and subcontractor requirements
- Audit requirements
- Intergovernmental review for federal grants
- Directions for completing grant assurances and application forms
- Board approval and signature requirements
- Budget form directions and funding requirements
- Stipulated attachments
- Final application preparation and checklist with timeline
- A contact name and phone number for questions

- Transmittal instructions including the number of grant copies required, how to address and prepare the grant materials for mailing, the deadline for receiving or mailing the grant, proof of mailing, and mail tracking requirements
- Grant proposal rating process, timeline, rating rubric, and evaluation criteria

Form 4.1 provides a sample form for designing a grant completion summary to meet a specific funder's specifications and requirements. Using the list above and a funder's grant proposal announcement and guidelines, create your own customized checklist for accurately completing all specified grant requirements. If you are uncertain about any of the requirements, create a list of questions and contact the funder for further clarification. Grant specifications can be compared to entering a contest. All rules and regulations must be followed to ensure maximum points and consideration.

SCHEDULING FUNDER INFORMATIONAL MEETINGS ■

After completely reviewing the grant proposal requirements, and summarizing the meeting schedule and grant specifications in Form 4.1, it is critical to determine the policies and procedures within the school district for completing the grant development process. Some school districts require that the grant development office and fiscal services review the grant application packet before attending grant informational meetings and planning to complete the grant. Other school districts require cabinet approval to proceed with writing a grant. Some districts allow schools to first write grants and then have them reviewed before submission.

When reviewing a grant's requirements, it is also critical to determine how many schools within a school district can apply for funding. Most grants require a superintendent's signature and some require board approval for submission. Check all of your district's requirements, policies, and procedures before progressing with your grant development plan. Always inform the superintendent's office that you are planning to apply to a specific funder for a grant. Too many teachers write their own grants and later discover that the district may have a conflict of interest with a particular funder or that the grant is too costly for the school district to manage.

Form 4.2 provides a means for identifying the key stakeholders that should be invited to grant informational meetings. Key stakeholders can include school district level administrators, grantwriters, program developers, board members, school site leadership team members, subcontractors, advocates, and parents.

Form 4.1. Grant Proposal Summary With Timeline

Program name and funder: _____

Summarize all grant specifications:_____

_____

_____

_____

_____

_____

List all informational grant meetings: _____

_____

_____

Describe all application format requirements and page limits: _____

_____

_____

List all forms to be completed with specific signature or board requirements: _____

_____

_____

List all attachments that must be included in the grant packet: _____

_____

_____

_____

Summarize the number of the grant copies required, the addressing and mailing requirements, and the date
and time the grant packet must be received:_____

_____

_____

_____

Summarize how the criteria will be used for funding the proposal:_____

_____

_____

_____

List any questions for the funder: _____

_____

_____

_____

_____

Funder Contact Name:_____ Phone Number: _____

Form 4.2. Schedule for Informational Meeting With Stakeholders

Program name and funder: _____

The following individuals should be included in the grant's informational meeting:

Meeting date:_____ Meeting time:_____ Meeting location: _____

Key Stakeholder's Contact Information	*Grant Development Role*
Name Phone number Address E-mail	
Name Phone number Address E-mail	
Name Phone number Address E-mail	

In the chart below, list all activities that must be completed by various stakeholders to complete the grant development process. Identify the date for each activity and determine who must be present to complete specific agenda activities. Determine who should participate in grant-training sessions, the program's needs' assessment, the program's development plan, the evaluation plan, the program budget, and the final review for signing the grant application.

Meeting Dates, Locations, and Agenda	Names and Phone Numbers of Attendees

CONVENING A GRANT
■ **NEEDS ASSESSMENT MEETING**

Needs assessment instruments can include in-depth interviews with key informants, focus groups of stakeholder groups with similar interests or demographic characteristics, focus groups of stakeholder groups representing diverse interests or demographic characteristics, survey instruments, telephone interviews, and an analysis of diverse demographic data. The collection of needs assessment data can seem overwhelming without a clear plan and timeline for data collection and analysis to meet the grant development timeline for completion. The easiest process for identifying the needs for a specific program is to first read the grant application packet carefully to determine what data are requested to establish a need for a specific program. Most grant applications request a combination of the following data to be collected and analyzed to determine the extent of need for a specific program:

- Demographic data about the community including ethnic composition, median household income, teen pregnancy rate, rates of substance abuse, crime and gang-related statistics, household composition, foster care data, homeless data, child abuse and neglect data, health care services, and educational attainment levels of adults

- School district and school site data including grade-level enrollment numbers, ethnic composition, English proficiency statistics, out-of-home placements, low-income statistics, graduation and dropout rates, college acceptance rates, standardized testing results, attendance rates, the number and types of health and human care service referrals and intervention services, and crime statistics

- School district and school site data on teacher credentials and support staff training

- School district and school site professional development training on the state curriculum frameworks and standards

- An analysis of the district's or school's current academic program and the need for professional development, family literacy training, cultural competency and academic support services, various health and human care support services, and community safety and after-school childcare services

Once the grant request requirements are reviewed, a grant template that includes needs assessment data should be created for all stakeholders to complete before convening a needs assessment meeting. Key themes that should be considered while completing the grant template include the following:

1. How will the proposed program respond to identified needs?

2. What capacity and experience does your staff have to create and deliver this program?

3. How cost effective is your program design for maximizing the delivery of services?

4. When, where, and what is the frequency service delivery?

A grant template can help the grantwriter (1) focus on the funder's proposal requirements, (2) facilitate and collect demographic and program data from diverse stakeholders, and (3) consolidate and edit input from diverse stakeholders' grant responses into a cohesive and well-researched grant document. Grant templates can be designed to include a grant proposal's introduction; the problem statement; the program with goals, objectives, activities, and a timeline; the organizational capacity and experience of staff; the evaluation plan; and the program sustainability plan. A detailed process for constructing the grant template is described and illustrated in Chapter 6.

Processes for conducting needs assessments for program development and expansion include (1) conducting brainstorming sessions with the participation of all stakeholders; (2) creating a Pareto chart that organizes the needs data in a checklist chart with the largest number of stakeholders identifying a need displayed in the left column and the smallest group displayed on the right as illustrated in Table 4.1; (3) constructing a flowchart to identify improvement opportunities gaps in service; (4) using a fishbone diagram to illustrate the causes and effects of various program solutions responding to needs; and (5) creating scatter charts, histograms, and other statistical applications.

FACILITATING A STAKEHOLDER MEETING FOR COMPLETING A WORKSHEET GRANT TEMPLATE ∎

Once a preliminary grant template has been designed to respond to all information requested by the funder, the school's leadership team must facilitate a meeting with all program stakeholders to complete the information requested in the grant template. The meeting can be organized in the following order and format:

1. All stakeholders should review the grant's request for proposal and timeline for completing various grant requirements.

2. The stakeholders must evaluate the preliminary grant template to determine if all information requested by the funder has been included in the various template components.

Table 4.1 Pareto Chart on Need for Expanded After-School Childcare Services Checklist Indicating the Number of Stakeholders Supporting Expanded Services

Increased Tutoring	Increased Sports	Test Taking Strategy Class	Field Trips	Self-Defense Training
111111111111	111111111111	111111111111	111111111111	111111
111111111111	111111111111	1111111	11	
111111111111	11			

NOTE: Each "1" listed in the table represents a stakeholder supporting expanded services.

3. Each stakeholder should complete the entire template or stakeholders can be broken into smaller groups to answer one part of the grant template. The time required to complete the entire grant template or template component will vary according to the amount of information required to complete the assigned template or component.

4. After 15 to 30 minutes of completing the template, small groups of stakeholders can discuss specific template components. Groups can be formed to discuss (1) the need statement, (2) the proposed program's design, (3) the school's capacity to provide services, (4) the evaluation plan to measure program outcomes, and (5) the proposed budget and plan for program sustainability. Each group must designate a recorder and a facilitator who will report back to the larger group the results of its discussion.

5. After the group completes its designated grant template component for 30 to 60 minutes, the group facilitator must summarize the group's recommendations that the recorder has summarized on the grant template form.

6. The school's leadership team will review each group's recommendations after the brainstorming meeting with all stakeholders is concluded. The leadership team will make any modifications required to streamline the services to be delivered in the program.

7. After the initial stakeholder brainstorming session and leadership team evaluation, the grantwriter will complete the first draft of the grant proposal.

8. After writing the first draft of the grant proposal, the grantwriter must identify (1) any missing information that must be further developed to complete the grantwriting process, (2) any duplication of data or services that must be further clarified, and (3) any gaps in the proposed program that must be filled.

9. After completing this analysis, the grantwriter must schedule and convene appropriate follow-up meetings.

CONVENING FOLLOW-UP MEETINGS FOR GRANT DEVELOPMENT AND IMPLEMENTATION ■

Creating a comprehensive grant program with various stakeholders and subcontractors can become overwhelming without a clear plan and timeline for completing the grant proposal process. Typically, after the funder information meeting and stakeholder brainstorming session are completed, the grantwriter can develop an overall marketing strategy for securing funding. The grantwriter's management of funder and diverse stakeholder relationships is critical for effective program development, successful funding, and full program implementation. It is imperative that the grantwriter organize any funder questions and define a grant development plan with a manageable timeline for completion. Table 4.2 provides a timeline of a sample grant process.

Without a clearly defined plan in place, challenges can occur that will impede the grant development process. The following is a summary of typical challenges that can occur during the grant development process:

Funder eligibility: The funder's informational meeting does not clearly specify district school sites that meet the funding criteria. When it is not clear which schools will meet the funder's requirements, it is critical that the school or district meet with the funder after the informational meeting to clarify specific schools that qualify for funding. Once specific eligible schools have been identified, it is imperative that the funder confirm in writing the recommended schools that can apply for funding before the district or the school proceeds with the grant development process.

District protocol: The applicant school has not followed the district's policies and procedures before submitting the grant to the funder. Whenever a school site administrator or central office grantwriter discovers that a staff member, teacher, or administrator has submitted a grant to a funder without appropriate approvals, the applicant school or district office must inform all appropriate authorities. An appropriate plan of action must be defined and pursued to secure funding and to have all stakeholders obtain the proper authorization and signatures.

Narrative guidelines: The funder's guidelines for completing the grant proposal's format, content, and process are not clear. Whenever further clarification of the grantwriting process is required, the grant applicant must

Table 4.2 Timeline of a Sample Grant Process

Timeline	Grant Process Activity
January 15, 20XX	• Review all grant specifications. • Schedule all funder information meetings with appropriate leaders and stakeholders. • Attend the funder's information meeting.
January 25, 20XX	• Create a grant worksheet template for all stakeholders to complete at the grant needs assessment meeting.
January 30, 20XX	• Convene a grant needs assessment meeting with all program stakeholders to identify program needs, program plans, and evaluation instruments.
February 7, 20XX	• Facilitate a stakeholder meeting to receive input on the various grant component sections and to complete the grant template. • Organize work teams to complete various grant sections by February 28, 20XX
February 28, 20XX	• Meet with work team leaders and key stakeholders to compile all information for the initial grant draft.
March 10, 20XX	• Complete the entire grant application and preliminary budget and review with key stakeholders and work team leaders for modification and edits.
March 13, 20XX	• Submit the final grant application to the school district administrators for final grant approval and signatures.
March 20, 20XX	• Make the required grant copies and mail through the U.S. mail to the funder to meet the grant application deadline of April 1, 20XX. • Distribute copies of the grant application packet to key stakeholders, school district administrators, and subcontractors.
April 1 – May 30, 20XX	• Track the grant submission process until final grant decisions are made.
June 1, 20XX	• Verify that the final grant notification has been mailed to funded applicants. When the grant notification letter has been received, mail the required documentation to the funder by the deadline. • Create a schedule for program implementation activities with key stakeholders, school district staff, and subcontractors.
July 1, 20XX	• Attend the grant award participant information meeting with the funder to learn how to implement the grant and to meet all funder's reporting requirements. • Create a schedule of all program reporting and financial reporting deadlines.
August 1, 20XX	• Meet with stakeholders and collaborators to identify other funding sources to enhance and expand the newly implemented program.

(1) review all grant guidelines; (2) create a list of all questions that must be answered by the funder for further clarification; and (3) contact the funder to have all questions answered for completing the grant proposal, required forms, and budget. The funder and applicant can also set up an appointment after the initial draft grant application is completed for a preliminary review to identify any areas that need further development. Some funders will be responsive to this request while other funders will be concerned about providing equitable technical support to all grant applicants. A few funders will only allow questions to be submitted in writing during a specific period of time. After the specified time, no technical support will be provided by the funder or no more grant proposal questions will be answered.

Collaborations: The funder requires that the applicant must share the delivery of services with other community-based organizations and school organizations. If a grant requires collaborations in the delivery of services, it is critical for the grant applicant to identify diverse community stakeholders and school organizations that can adequately support and provide appropriate services. Prospective community partners can be identified from

- Health and human care social service agencies
- A regional database that lists local and regional health and human care agencies
- A local United Way agency
- References available at the local library
- Resources available from state and county school associations
  - Web searches
  - Agencies that have effectively served your students or that have provided previous services

Once a list of prospective partners is developed, all should be contacted to determine if they can provide appropriate services at reasonable costs that will meet the grant's guidelines for funding and service delivery.

Fiscal agent: The district or school does not have adequate staffing, program resources, or service delivery capacity to meet the grant's requirements. When reviewing the various requirements for creating a program, preliminary budgets should be created to determine the proposed costs for various problem solutions. When it is determined that the school district's or school's usage of internal staffing or resources may be too costly, the school or district must research the feasibility of using community-based subcontractors to deliver various program service components. It is typically becoming more cost-effective to have subcontractors provide school-based childcare services, school lunch programs, janitorial services, computer maintenance services, and school site and school district business management services. The school and district must consider which subcontractor or internal department can best support the needs of the school's or district's diverse student populations within the limitations and guidelines of a specific grant program.

Budget matches: The applicant school does not have sufficient resources to meet the fiscal match requirement. Whenever program delivery fiscal matches are required from funders, it is critical to coordinate the budget's development through the school district's fiscal services department to limit any errors in identifying appropriate fiscal matches to meet a grant's budget requirements. Typically, school sites tend to list district and school site matches that cannot be used for a specific grant. For example, some states do not allow schools to use other state-funded resources for matches; however, federal and county funds for various budget categories can be used. Always verify all allocated fiscal budget matches with an authorized fiscal services department employee for accuracy.

5

Integral Grant Proposal Components

Most federal, state, local, and foundation grants include the following proposal components:

- The grant's introduction

- The problem and needs statement

- The program design with clearly defined goals, objectives, and activities with a timeline

- The organizational capacity and experience of staff

- The evaluation plan

- The program's budget and budget narrative

- The program's plan for sustainability beyond the grant funding cycle

How each grant component is presented to the funder will have a direct impact on funding. Therefore, it is critical to consider the various strategies a grantwriter can use for creating grant components that are (1) responsive to the information the funder needs to know to adequately evaluate the grant proposal, (2) integrative and support all other proposal components in the problem solution and in the program strategies for responding to the problem, and (3) appropriate for responding to the unique contextual needs of a specific community and client population.

Many funders have created rubric charts for evaluating each grant proposal. These charts are usually included in the grant proposal information packet. As the grantwriting team creates each grant component, it is vital to refer to the rubric for that component to determine if the information being compiled is responsive to the funder's rubric for adequately addressing what has been requested for a specific grant component. The following sections describe and provide suggestions for developing the key grant components requested in most proposals from diverse funding sources.

■ THE GRANT'S INTRODUCTION

The introduction provides a brief overview of the proposed problem with an explanation of how a school district or school intends to respond to the problem. The proposed program should focus on briefly answering the informational questions of who, what, when, where, why, and how in its proposed problem solution. Box 5.1 provides a sample grant introduction for an after-school childcare and academic enrichment program. Table 5.1 provides an analysis of how the sample grant introduction paragraph provides an overview of the proposed problem and briefly answers the informational questions of who, what, when, where, why, and how in its proposed problem solution. Form 5.1 provides a sample grant introduction form. Chapter 6 describes and illustrates how grantwriters can create customized grant template narratives that respond to specific funders' grant proposal questions and requirements.

■ THE PROBLEM AND NEEDS STATEMENT

The grant's problem and needs statement provides a contextual documented description about the problem or need to be addressed. The needs statement provides the justification to funders for requesting specific project funding. It defines the significance of a problem and proposes appropriate solutions to the problem in relation to a community's and a specific population's need. An effective problem and needs statement links various program components to documented needs with successfully proven research strategies for problem resolution. Effective needs statements should include answers to the following questions to help the funder become more contextually sensitive to the unique circumstances surrounding a school community's need:

1. What problem or need are you trying to solve?
2. What is the extent of the problem?
3. Why should this problem be solved?

Box 5.1

**Sample Grant Introduction
for an After-School Childcare
and Academic Enrichment Program**

United Elementary School District, located in south central Los Angeles, requests $350,000 for start-up and 3 years of program funding to create and develop an on-site comprehensive after-school childcare and academic enrichment program to serve its 1,500 K-5 low-income, culturally diverse, primarily limited English-proficient student population. The school currently does not provide any on-site after-school childcare, academic enrichment, tutorial support, or heath and human care services for students and their families.

The proposed program will partner with the We Care Child Development Agency to provide on-site Monday through Friday after-school childcare services from 3:00 p.m. until 6:00 p.m. to 200 low income primarily K-3 students. The Academic Solutions tutoring agency will provide after-school reading and math tutorial services to 400 low-income K-5 students for a 1-hour session twice a week for 15 weeks. Academic enrichment and community partners will provide daily nutritional snacks to all student participants, in addition to organized sports teams, performing arts activities, hobby clubs, computer training, and field trips. Families of the students will receive training in parent education, family literacy, computer skill development, and vocational skill development. Social workers will provide families with appropriate referrals for basic needs services, health care, family counseling, and job referral support services.

---

4. What community demographics and factors contribute to this problem?

5. How do the community's demographics support the problem and need?

6. What makes this problem significantly more relevant within your community?

7. What is the impact of this problem in your community compared to other similar communities?

8. What capacity does the community have to respond to the problem?

9. What program models are adequately responding to this need?

10. Who are the community stakeholders that have expertise in responding to this problem?

11. Who can you collaborate with to streamline the delivery of services?

Table 5.1 Analysis of the Sample Grant Introduction Paragraph

Component	Text That Responds to the Information Requested
Problem overview	United Elementary School District, located in south central Los Angeles, requests $350,000 for start-up and 3 years of program funding to create and develop an on-site comprehensive after-school childcare and academic enrichment program to serve its 1,500 K-5 low-income, culturally diverse, primarily limited English-proficient students population. The school currently does not provide any on-site after-school childcare, academic enrichment, tutorial support, or heath and human care services for students and their families.
Who?	200 of the school's K-3 students will receive childcare services from the We Care Child Development Agency; 400 K-5 students will receive tutoring; and all participants and their families will receive academic enrichment and support services.
What?	We Care Child Development Agency will provide Monday through Friday after-school childcare services from 3:00 p.m. until 6:00 p.m. to 200 low-income primarily K-3 students. The Academic Solutions tutoring agency will provide after-school reading and math tutorial services to 400 low-income K-5 students for a 1-hour session twice a week for 15 weeks. Academic enrichment and community partners will provide daily nutritional snacks to all student participants, in addition to organized sports teams, performing arts activities, hobby clubs, computer training, and field trips. Families of the students will be able to receive training in parent education, family literacy, computer skill development, and vocational skill development. Social workers will provide families with appropriate referrals for basic needs services, health care, family counseling, and job referral support services.
When?	Childcare services will be provided Monday through Friday from 3:00 p.m. until 6:00 p.m. After-school reading and math tutorial services will be provided for a 1-hour session twice a week for 15 weeks. All other services will be planned monthly and by individual appointments for family support services and referrals.
Where?	All direct services will take place at the school site. Referral services will be offered at the referred agency sites.
Why?	The school currently does not provide any on-site after-school childcare, academic enrichment, tutorial support, or heath and human care services for students and their families.
How?	We Care Child Development Agency will provide on-site after-school childcare services. The Academic Solutions tutoring agency will provide on-site after-school reading and math tutorial services. Academic enrichment and community partners will provide all other program services and referrals.

Form 5.1. Sample Grant Introduction Form

Component	*Text That Responds to the Information Requested*
Problem overview	
Who?	
What?	
When?	
Where?	
Why?	
How?	

Table 5.2 lists the various types of data that can be collected with possible strategies and resources available for identifying or compiling the data. Table 5.3 provides a sample of the various types and sources of data that can be collected for developing an after-school childcare and enrichment program at a school site. Form 5.2 provides a sample form that can help the grantwriter identify appropriate data and sources that must be collected to complete a grant's needs statement.

THE PROGRAM DESIGN WITH GOALS, OBJECTIVES, ACTIVITIES, AND A TIMELINE

Most funders require that the proposed program include goals with objectives, activities, and a timeline. Goals are broad statements that indicate the overall intent and desired change from the proposed program. Objectives refer to the changes that will occur as a result of an intervention and are concrete statements that are specific, measurable, attainable, related to a target population, and time sensitive. Process objectives measure changes in a process to achieve specific program results. Output objectives describe the types or units of services provided to a specific number of clients. Outcome objectives describe the changes in behavior and/or expected benefits to a specific numbers of clients or within an organization. The time interval for achieving an outcome can be initial or startup, intermediate or short term, and ultimate or long term. Activities refer to the processes that bring objectives to fruition. Specific program activities within a time frame can support the completion of process objectives and the achievable results of outcome objectives. Using the after-school childcare program example used in previous sections, Box 5.2 and Tables 5.4-5.6 illustrate how program goals, different types of program objectives, and timelines can be included in the following program plan formats:

- A grant's program narrative as demonstrated in Box 5.2
- A program workplan form as modeled in Table 5.4
- A scope of work contract form provided in Table 5.5
- A GANTT chart that lists specific activities in relation to a calendar of months or quarters during the entire project duration as displayed in Table 5.6

Forms 5.3 and 5.4 include a workplan form and GANTT chart to assist the grantwriter in developing the program narrative.

THE ORGANIZATIONAL CAPACITY AND EXPERIENCE OF STAFF

The school's capacity for delivering services as well as the qualifications of key program staff are vital for the program's success. If the school and

(text continues on p. 62)

Table 5.2 Types of Needs Statement Data and Sources

Data Type	Data Indicator	Data Source
Community profile	Location, history, population, ethnicity Income, employment data, and composition of household Health statistics, number of foster placements Rate of homelessness Crime and domestic violence data	City and county reports City and state database and census data County data County data City and county data
School district profile	Student enrollment by school and grade Percentage of various ethnic groups Percentage of low income or free lunches Percentage limited English proficient Dropout and college placement rates Crime reporting data	District and state database District and state database District and county database District and state database District and state database District and state database
School profile	Description of services, programs, policies, and procedures	School district, handbook, and policies
Student profile	Student enrollment by grade Percentage of various ethnic groups Percentage of low income or free lunches Percentage limited English proficient Dropout and college placement rates Number in various programs and services Specific student characteristics	District and state database District and state database District and county database District and state database District and state database District and state database Interviews and focus groups
County, state, and national comparisons	All demographic data Proven program strategies Financial allocation distributions	State and federal databases Grant annual reports Program budget reports
Program models	Proven program strategies Recommended program model with specific goals, objectives, timeline	Diverse funder models Description in a funder's proposal
Proven collaborative partners	Current service providers at the school or district, or community collaborative partners Providers for similar programs or collaborative partnerships	School and district database Referrals from other schools and districts
Proven evaluation models	In-depth interviews, focus groups, survey completions, telephone interviews, demonstrations Test score data, student portfolios, journals, logs, meeting minutes Cost effectiveness and benefit analysis	Program participants and key stakeholder groups Data collected from the school, district, and partners District fiscal services

Table 5.3 Sample After-School Childcare Needs Statement Data and Sources

Data Type	Data Indicator	Data Source
Community profile	Overall demographic data including the number of students needing childcare and current gaps in community services	Community and county reports and database analysis
School district profile	Number of students, ethnicity, percentage of low income, percentage limited English proficient, data on academic performance and needs	School and district database, reports, and in-depth interviews
School profile	Participation and types of current programs and specific needs	School data, reports, and in-depth interviews
Student profile	Number of students, ethnicity, percentage of low income, percentage limited English proficient, data on academic performance and needs	School and district database, reports, and in-depth interviews
State and national comparisons	Gaps of services locally, regionally, statewide, and nationally	State and national databases and reports
Program models	An analysis of current models with evaluation and outcomes	State, national databases, reports, and funder reports
Proven collaborative partners	Listing of current partners from school, district, similar districts, and funders	Databases from districts, the state, and funders
Proven evaluation models	Instruments include interviews, focus groups, surveys, intake logs, academic performance, and parent employment	National, state, county, and funder model reports

Form 5.2. Sample Needs Statement Data and Sources Form

Data Type	Data Indicator	Data Source
Community profile		
School district profile		
School profile		
Student profile		
County, state, and national comparisons		
Program models		
Proven collaborative partners		
Proven evaluation models		

Box 5.2

Sample After-School Childcare Program Narrative

Goal statement:

To provide on-site after-school childcare to 200 low-income primarily K-3 students from Monday to Friday from 3:00 p.m. until 6:00 p.m.

Initial or startup process objective:

By June 30, 20XX, United Elementary School District will contract with the We Care Child Development Agency to provide Monday through Friday on-site after-school childcare services to 200 low-income primarily K-3 students as demonstrated by the completed and signed contract between the school district and the contracting agency.

Program activities with timeline:

1. The project coordinator will contact the We Care Child Development Agency and schedule three meeting dates to complete the contract negotiations process from May 15, 20XX through June 30, 20XX.

2. In preparation of the first meeting, the project coordinator will meet with the school district's contract services manager to draft a preliminary contract based on the specifications of the grant and the school district's contract development policies and procedures by May 25, 20XX.

3. After the second meeting with the contractor, the project director will update the contract based on the contractor's feedback and resubmit to the contract services manager for preliminary approval by June 15, 20XX.

4. After the third meeting, the project director will verify that all authorized individuals have signed all contracts and the project manager will prepare the school board motion report to approve the signed contract at the June 30 Board meeting.

---

school district can demonstrate to the funder that they have the facility, the resources, the experience, and the trained staffing to support the proposed program, the funder will be confident that the program can be effectively implemented. When a school is lacking in specific service delivery experiences required for the program, the school and school district should form collaborative partnerships with community-based organizations that can demonstrate significant experience in areas of program need. A school's previous experience with the targeted population will also assure the funder of effective program development.

(text continues on p. 68)

Table 5.4 Sample After-School Childcare Program Workplan

Goal #1		
To provide on-site after-school childcare to 200 low-income primarily K-3 students, Monday to Friday from 3:00 p.m. until 6:00 p.m.		
Output Intermediate Objectives	*Activities*	*Time*
1.1: By June 30, 20XX, United Elementary School District will complete its first year contract with the We Care Child Development Agency to provide Monday through Friday on-site after-school childcare services to a total of 200 low-income primarily K-3 students as demonstrated by the initial registration of 100 students by September 30, 20XX and as docu-mented in the program's registration records.	1.1: Complete the contract negotiation process with the We Care Child Development Agency.	5/20XX-6/20XX
	1.2: Create the childcare registration process and marketing campaign.	6/20XX-7/20XX
	1.3: Market, recruit, and register the first 100 students for the program.	8/20XX
	1.4: Document the number of students registered for the program by counting the number of students registered.	9/20XX
2.1: By September 30, 20XX, a total of 60 hours of childcare services will be provided to 100 students as documented in the program's daily log-in sheets.	2.1: Complete the plan for documenting student atten-dance during the contract negotiation.	5/20XX-6/20XX
	2.2: Verify the log-in sheets to determine the number of hours each student participated in the program.	9/20XX

Table 5.5 Sample After-School Childcare Program Scope of Work Contract

---

Organization: United Elementary School District

Project name: Childcare Program

Goal #1: To provide on-site after-school childcare to 200 low-income primarily K-3 students, Monday to Friday from 3:00 p.m. until 6:00 p.m.

Outcome objective: By June 30, 20XX, 200 low-income primarily K-3 students attending the United Elementary School District's K-5 school will receive safe and secure on-site after-school childcare services provided by We Care Child Development Agency.

Outcome measurements: The program's registration records will provide documentation to support the number of appropriate students registered in the program, and district safety reports, focus groups, and in-depth interviews with diverse stakeholders will document if the program provided a safe and secure environment.

Staff	Project Activities	Timeline	Evaluation Process
Project director	1.1: Complete the contract negotiation process with the agency.	5/20XX–6/20XX	Signed contract and completed process
We Care	1.2: Create the childcare registration process and marketing campaign.	6/20XX–7/20XX	Registration forms and campaign
Staff project director	1.3: Market, recruit, and register 200 students for the program.	Monthly	Completed registrations
	1.4: Document the number of students in the program by counting the number registered and determining if the program provided a safe and secure environment.	Quarterly	Registration forms document count; safety reports interviews / focus groups for safety

Table 5.6 Sample After-School Childcare Program GANTT Chart

Goal #1: To provide on-site after-school childcare to 200 low-income primarily K-3 students, Monday to Friday from 3:00 p.m. until 6:00 p.m.

Outcome objective: By June 30, 20XX, 200 low-income primarily K-3 students attending the United Elementary School District's K-5 school will receive safe and secure on-site after-school childcare services provided by We Care Child Development Agency.

Activity	*5/20XX– 8/20XX*	*8/20XX– 11/20XX*	*12/20XX– 3/20XX*	*4/20XX– 7/20XX*
Complete the contract negotiation process with the agency.	X			
Create the childcare registration process and marketing campaign.	X			
Market, recruit, and register 200 students for the program.	X	X	X	X
Document the number of students in the program by counting the number registered and determining through safety reports, interviews, and focus groups if the program provided a safe and secure environment.	X	X	X	X

Form 5.3. Sample Workplan Form

Goal #1		
Output Intermediate Objectives	*Activities*	*Time*
1.1:	1.1: 1.2: 1.3: 1.4:	
2.1:	2.1: 2.2: 2.3: 2.4:	

Form 5.4. Sample GANTT Chart

Goal #1:				
Outcome objective:				
Activity	*5/20XX– 8/20XX*	*8/20XX– 11/20XX*	*12/20XX– 3/20XX*	*4/20XX– 7/20XX*

The following factors can have a significant impact on successful program outcomes:

- The facility's location, maintenance services, layout, space, and current rate of usage
- The facility's accessibility to the client community, staffing, and other service delivery community partners
- The ownership of or ability to secure capital equipment, supplies, books, duplicating machines, computers, and telephone services to support the program
- The appropriate training, skill development, and experience of school site administrators, teachers, and staff to support the program
- The ethnic experience, linguistic ability, and cultural sensitivity of staff in working with the targeted school community
- The governance and organizational structure of the school and the school district to support various program components
- The equipment, skills, and technical support to develop appropriate evaluation instruments and data management systems to collect data to measure outcomes
- The availability of community support, collaborators, and subcontractors to support program components that the district cannot adequately or economically provide
- Documentation of the school district's and school's past performance in providing similar services including annual program reports, public relations materials, press releases, awards, and honors

Table 5.7 provides a sample organizational capacity and experience of staff assessment and Form 5.5 provides a sample organizational capacity and experience of staff assessment form to assist the grantwriter in determining the school's and school district's credibility capacity for funder support.

■ THE EVALUATION PLAN

The evaluation plan should include a systematic process of collecting data that measures the completion of program objectives through achievable results and outcomes. A process evaluation focuses on the procedures used for developing the program. An outcome evaluation determines how effectively a program has achieved its objectives. Unlike research, grant evaluation plans are designed to support decision-making purposes. Evaluations can also be viewed as formative or summative. Formative evaluations support decision making while the program is operating under the funder's funding cycle, whereas

Table 5.7 Sample Organizational Capacity and Experience of Staff Assessment

Factor	*Capacity and / or Experience*
The facility's structure and usage	The United Elementary School District After-School Childcare and Academic Enrichment program site is located on the K-5 school site. The site has been renovated to support an extensive childcare and enrichment program for 200 K-3 childcare participants and for 400 K-5 after-school reading and math tutorial students.
The facility's access to the targeted population	The facility is located on the school grounds where the targeted population attends school from Monday through Friday.
Capital equipment, services, and supplies	The after-school facility is fully equipped to support the targeted population with childcare and tutorial services. Nutritional snacks are provided by the service providers. Families participating in various program components will have access to the supplies provided by the program.
Staff training and experience	The program staff is fully credentialed in their area of expertise and each staff member has 3-5 years of working experiences.
Ethnic, linguistic, and cultural experience	All program staff can speak a second language (i.e., Spanish and Chinese) due to the large number of limited English proficient students who speak these languages. The language proficiency, ethnic, and cultural experiences of the staff reflect the ethnic, linguistic, and cultural experiences of the clients.
The governance and organizational structure	The United Elementary School District will serve as the project's fiscal agent. The district's K-5 school site principal and leadership team will manage the project for the district. Each subcontracting agency will have a site-based project manager who will coordinate its program component with the school's principal.
Evaluation instruments and data collection	Childcare intake logs will track the number and hours of service delivery. All families and students participating in the program will complete pre- and post-knowledge-based surveys each quarter on the various educational concepts that have been presented to students and their families. Quarterly focus groups and interviews will be conducted to validate the information collected through the surveys and to evaluate which program components may need further modification to meet the changing needs of the program's participants.
Documentation of past performance	A data tracking database will be created to track and collect all information compiled from the intake logs, surveys, focus groups, and interviews. Quarterly reports will be generated to track the data that have been collected.
Other	Yearly reports will be created on the project to present to funders, community collaborators, and the press for documentation and for the program's further development.

Form 5.5. Sample Organizational Capacity and Experience of Staff Assessment Form

Factor	Capacity and/or Experience
The facility's structure and usage	
The facility's access to the targeted population	
Capital equipment, services, and supplies	
Staff training and experience	
Ethnic, linguistic and cultural experience	
The governance and organizational structure	
Evaluation instruments and data collection	
Documentation of past performance	
Other	

summative evaluations are reserved for the time when a decision must be made to continue an intervention after a funding cycle has been completed. Hence, it is essential that the grantwriter identify evaluation stakeholders to ascertain what each stakeholder views as credible evidence. The grantwriter must document the specific results these important stakeholders expect for the intervention in general, immediately, and at the end of the funding cycle. The collected evidence must be identified to determine whether the program achieved its objectives. Funders may also request measures of program implementation. These measures document whether the intervention was implemented as intended. If the implementation was incomplete or different than described in the project's workplan, the grantwriter must explain the conditions and reasons for any modification.

Evaluations can be conducted by project staff as well as by outside evaluators. Typically, external evaluation consultants evaluate large federally funded grants. By using an outside evaluator at the beginning of the grant development process, the grant evaluation plan can adequately evaluate the results of the program to increase accountability. Outside evaluators can be recruited through local universities as well as through funder referrals of evaluators who are currently evaluating similar programs. Depending on the evaluation design and time requirements to complete the evaluation plan, some evaluators can serve as advisors or program auditors for a 1- or 2-day consultation fee. These consultants can determine if the evaluation plan is valid and ensure that adequate measures of the intervention's implementation are included and clearly defined in the plan. Federal agencies typically require an accountability report that a project officer has checked off to be certain that all components have been covered. Foundations generally request short reports that are based on personal contacts and rapport between the project officer and the project coordinator. As part of the grant evaluation process, a funder may contract with an external evaluator to manage all the funder's grant evaluations in a particular program. The cost for this type of evaluation is usually included as part of the program funding allocation.

Internal evaluators employed by the school or school district can evaluate smaller foundation or government programs. Regardless of the type of evaluator used to support the evaluation process, it is critical that the grantwriter acquires expertise in determining how to best evaluate various types of program objectives. The following benefits can occur for the school and the school community through the systematic evaluation of project data collected:

- The school and school district can better understand the needs of their target population through an analysis of various demographic characteristics.

- The school and school district can understand what factors in a school community may have a direct impact on the program's results.

- Systematic contextual data analysis can help a school or school district determine what specific activities must be modified or incorporated in the project's development to achieve the proposed outcomes.

- The school and school district can use the data to strategically plan additional program components to support previously unidentified needs and gaps in service delivery.

- The school and school district can use the data to streamline service delivery and identify collaborative partners and subcontractors who can support previously unmet needs.

- The school and school district can identify program areas that can leverage new and added funding from community and governmental funders.

- Evaluation program results can be used for public relations purposes to garner community support and added resources for other programs.

Funders can also benefit from a school or school district's evaluation of a grant program in the following ways:

- As systematic data evaluations are submitted to the funder, the funder can identify what program components are specifically working and not working.

- Through this continuous feedback, the funder can provide the project site staff with appropriate technical support and guidance on how to overcome challenges and how to better meet the target population's needs addressed in the program's objectives.

- Project sites that demonstrate success in their program evaluation can be used as demonstration sites and provide technical support to newly funded projects.

- The data collected from various project sites can be used to leverage more community interest and funding to respond to a specific educational need.

- The data collected from various project sites can be used for legislative lobbying for policy development and funding to support a particular educational need, strategy, or reform initiative.

- The data collected from program evaluations can be used for the funder's public relations campaigns.

The process for creating an evaluation plan includes (1) identifying the program objectives that must be measured, (2) determining what types of data must be collected to measure the completion of a process or an achievable result, (3) creating a process with a timeline for collecting and analyzing the data that have been collected, and (4) creating a plan with identified staffing of how the data will be collected, analyzed, and reported to various program stakeholders for continuous improvement and to the funder to comply with all funding requirements and deadlines. Table 5.8 displays examples of different objective evaluation instruments to measure the completed and achievable results of various process, output, and outcome objectives. Form 5.6 provides a sample evaluation plan form for the grantwriter to use in creating the grant's evaluation plan.

THE PROGRAM'S BUDGET AND BUDGET NARRATIVE ■

The grant budget should include all program expenditures to support a program's staffing, benefits, books, supplies, services and other operating expenditures, capital outlay, miscellaneous outgo, and administrative overhead. Funders typically limit the percentage requested to support administrative overhead for the project. Most funders use three different budget types: (1) the simplified line item program budget, (2) the functional program budget, and (3) the total organizational budget reported by category with a separate column listing funding requested by expenditure for the proposed grant program. The simplified line item budget includes the expenditures from specific budget categories. A functional budget lists expenditures within a program by function or service to be delivered. The total organizational budget provides the funder with a complete financial picture of the school's or school district's revenue and expenditures in relation to the categorical amounts being requested to fund a specific program.

Most budgets also request that the grant applicant include sources of other or matched funding. Matched funding can be secured through other types of grant sources specified by the funder, through fundraising events, program service fees, and program donations. Some funders request in-kind contributions to be reported in a special column in the budget. In-kind contributions can include volunteer time allocated to the project and donated supplies, services, and space. In-kind donations cannot be allocated to other grant programs. Each in-kind contribution must be determined by identifying the fair market value for the service being rendered or for the item being donated. All in-kind contribution valuations should be verified for accuracy through the school's or school district's fiscal services department.

The budget narrative will specifically describe how individual expenditures were calculated to determine the total for each budget category. Table 5.9 illustrates a proposed program simplified line item budget using the childcare program example and includes a variation of budget categories typically found on federal, state, and private foundation budget forms. Box 5.4 describes the types of expenses that can be

Table 5.8 Examples of Different Objective Evaluation Instruments

Evaluation Instruments	Process Objectives (How did it happen?)	Output Objectives (What quantity?)	Outcome Objectives (What changed?)
Demographic	Client background Staffing background	Number served Ethnicity of clients Client income levels	Client data changes Staffing data changes
Performance, standardized testing, and authentic assessments	Workplan status Training developed Materials developed Evaluation developed Program efficiency	Units of service Material disseminated Number trained Number tested Number participating	Achievement changes Attendance changes Dropout changes Increased college entry Portfolio improvement
Survey types	Satisfaction	Verify output totals	Attitudinal changes Pre- and postknowledge
Interviews and observations	Behavior changes Procedure changes	Verify output totals	Behavior changes Pre- and postknowledge
Focus groups	Verify growth Check perceptions	Verify output totals	Verify survey results Identify strengths Brainstorm solutions

Form 5.6. Sample Evaluation Plan Form

Type of Objective	Evaluation Instruments Selected With the Timeline and Person Responsible for Data Collection and Analysis
Process Objective #1: Process Objective #2: Process Objective #3:	
Output Objective #1: Output Objective #2: Output Objective #3:	
Outcome Objective #1: Outcome Objective #2: Outcome Objective #3:	

included in each budget category with the budget narrative for the budget in Box 5.3. Forms 5.7 and 5.8 provide sample budget and budget narrative forms.

■ THE PROGRAM'S PLAN FOR SUSTAINABILITY

Once the budget and budget narrative are completed, the grantwriting team must create a comprehensive fund development plan to sustain the program beyond the funding cycle. Funding options can include generating funding from other grant sources that are in compliance with a specific grant's requirements. Funds, contributions, and in-kind gifts can also be leveraged from the following diverse stakeholders and funding sources:

- Community-based organizations
- Businesses
- Other governmental sources
- Private foundation sources
- Corporate sponsorships
- Event planning and various types of fundraising activities

As the program receives more visibility and recognition in the community, other program delivery agencies and community-based services can be identified that may be able to support the program beyond its initial funding. Typically, a youth development organization can be contracted with to provide new and expanded after-school enrichment programs at school sites. Once a program is fully developed at a school site, it is fiscally beneficial for a community-based agency to create a satellite program at the school. By expanding its service delivery to a school site, a community-based organization can benefit in the following ways:

1. A previously developed program by school site staff can provide the community-based organization with a significant number of clients who are used to conforming to a grant funder's service delivery accountability requirements.

2. A school site program will offer a community agency a more diverse student population than it may have access to typically in its service delivery.

3. A community-based organization can coordinate services with students' teachers. For example, a school's teachers can provide tutorial support training and services to a community-based organization that is operating an on-site after-school tutoring program.

(text continues on p. 81)

Box 5.3

Sample After-School Childcare Program Simplified Line Item Budget

Budget Category	*Requested Funding*
1. Personnel salaries: • Full-time program coordinator • 15 child aides	$127,500
2. Employee benefits: • Full-time coordinator 25% of salary	$15,000
3. Supplies, books, and equipment: • $100 per student	$20,000
4. Contractual services, travel, and conferences: • 2 conferences for coordinator • 1 conference for 15 child aides	$1,900
5. Capital outlay: • 1 computer and printer	$1,200
6. Total direct costs (Lines 1-5):	$165,600
7. Indirect costs (10% of total direct costs):	$16,560
8. Total costs (Lines 6 + 7):	$182,160

Box 5.4

**Sample After-School Childcare
Expense Category Descriptions and Budget Narrative Form**

Line 1: Personnel salaries

Includes all certificated administrative and teachers' salaries, all classified personnel salaries, and other classified salaries.

- Full-time program coordinator @ $60,000 per year
- 15 child aides, $10 per hour x 15 hours per week x 30 weeks = $67,500

Line 2: Employee benefits

Includes all benefits for all staffing classifications. Employee benefits may include contributions to retirement plans, health and welfare benefits, contributions to social security, state unemployment insurance, and workers' compensation insurance.

- Full-time coordinator @ $60,000 annual salary x 25% representing the benefit rate for the school district = $15,000

Line 3: Supplies, books, and equipment

Includes all textbooks, program supplies, materials, and equipment to deliver the program.

- $100 in program supplies per year x 200 students = $20,000

Line 4: Contractual services, travel, and conferences

Includes all subcontractor expenditures and all necessary expenses incurred for travel and conferences.

- Coordinator: 2 conferences x 4 participants x $50 per event = $400
- 15 child aides: 1 conference x 15 participants x $100 registration fee = $1,500

Line 5: Capital outlay

Includes all expenditures for the project site, site improvement, office equipment, and furnishings that are not part of the permanent building structure.

- Quantity of 1 computer @ $800
- Quantity of 1 printer @ $400

Line 6: Total direct costs (Lines 1-5)

- $127,500 salaries + $15,000 benefits + $20,000 supplies + $1,900 conferences + $1,200 capital outlay = $165,600 total direct costs

Line 7: Indirect costs

- 10% x $165,600 = $16,560

Line 8: Total costs (Lines 6 + 7)

- $165,600 total direct costs + $16,560 indirect costs = $182,160 total costs

Form 5.7. Sample Budget Form

Budget Category	*Requested Funding*
Personnel salaries:	
Employee benefits:	
Supplies, books, and equipment:	
Contractual services, travel, and conferences:	
Capital outlay:	
Total direct costs (Lines 1-5):	
Indirect costs:	
Total costs (Lines 6 + 7):	

Form 5.8. Sample Budget Narrative Form

Line 1: Personnel salaries

Line 2: Employee benefits

Line 3: Supplies, books, and equipment

Line 4: Contractual services, travel, and conferences

Line 5: Capital outlay

Line 6: Total direct costs (Lines 1-5)

Line 7: Indirect costs

Line 8: Total costs (Lines 6 + 7)

4. The community agency will qualify for a wider variety of funding options by operating programs at a school site.

5. Data collection and accountability will be more accessible through a school site because the school is required to collect extensive demographic and academic achievement data to receive ongoing funding and academic accreditation.

Form 5.9 provides a sample program sustainability workplan for the grantwriter to use for identifying short- and long-term fundraising and subcontractor strategies to support the grant program beyond the funding cycle.

Form 5.9. Sample Program Sustainability Workplan

Specific Program Component	Current Allocation	Future Program Needs	Funding Strategy and Sources
		Short term: Long term:	Short term strategy: Long term strategy: Prospective funders:
		Short term: Long term:	Short term strategy: Long term strategy: Prospective funders:
		Short term: Long term:	Short term strategy: Long term strategy: Prospective funders:

6

Designing a Responsive Grant Template

Most funders request different types of information to be reported in their specific grant proposals. To meet diverse funder needs, a grantwriter can create a customized grant template that responds to a funder's proposal specifications. A grant template with supporting tables can be constructed to summarize data for specific grant components. For example, a grant table can be created to summarize a program need's supporting data; the proposed program goals, objectives, and timeline; the evaluation plan; the organization's experience in providing specific services; and a program sustainability plan. Grant templates can be organized according to specific funder guidelines. The template can assist the grantwriter when (1) facilitating needs assessment and program development sessions with diverse stakeholder groups, (2) assigning various grant components to different staff members for completion, and (3) consolidating and editing the various sections into a cohesive and well-documented grant proposal. The grantwriter can use the following 11 process steps to create a customized and responsive grant template:

1. Review all information that a funder is requesting in a specific proposal request.

2. Review the grant proposal's evaluation worksheet, the score summary sheet, or the proposal scoring rubric to identify the key grant components that will be evaluated for funding.

3. Review the factors that will be considered for each selection criteria that will be used for evaluating the grant.

4. Identify the relative scoring weights for each program selection criteria. For example, an introduction statement may be weighted at 10 points, the needs statement may also have a weighted score of 10, the quality and program design may have a weighted score of 40, the organization's capacity may have a score of 10, the evaluation plan may have a score of 20, and the budget and program sustainability plan may have a weighted score of 10 with a total program selection criteria weighted score of 100.

5. Construct the grant template in response to the grant's program-selection criteria.

6. Assist key stakeholders in formulating substantive responses to the grant's program selection criteria.

7. Edit diverse stakeholders' comments to represent the overall needs and proposed program components of all program stakeholders.

8. Identify evaluation tools and construct a plan that adequately measures results.

9. Use all stakeholders' feedback to formulate the final grant proposal for submission.

10. Create a budget that supports the program plan with a budget narrative that clearly articulates the costs of various services and a program sustainability plan for ongoing financial support beyond the grant's funding duration.

11. Create a follow-up plan with timeline for tracking funding and development.

The following sections describe and illustrate the process for coordinating and creating a responsive grant template using a large grant development team of key stakeholders and community collaborators.

STEP 1: REVIEWING ALL INFORMATION FOR A GRANT'S DEVELOPMENT

When the grantwriter first receives the funder's request for proposal packet, it is important for the grantwriter to read the entire packet first to determine the overall focus of the grant and to identify what the grantwriter must do to complete the grant development process. After reading the entire packet, the grantwriter should organize the funder's various grant requirements into an action plan that will do the following:

- Support the construction of the grant template
- Help stakeholders provide feedback on the various template components
- Create a timeline for completing each grant component in the development process

Form 6.1 provides a sample form for the grantwriter to use for organizing the template design process.

STEP 2: REVIEWING THE GRANT'S SCORING FORMS ■

Most funders include variations of grant scoring forms or rubrics to aid the grantwriter in determining the following questions:

- How the grant proposal should be prepared for the grant submission process
- What selection criteria will be used for funding recommendations
- What the relative scoring weights are for each program selection criterion

Forms 6.2 and 6.3, and Table 6.1 illustrate three different scoring instruments used by funders for evaluation. Form 6.2 lists the primary funder evaluation categories with descriptions of evaluation review strategies for each category. Form 6.3 lists the various scoring components and scoring ranges that a funder will use for funding recommendations. Table 6.1 provides a 4-point rubric for various key program components.

STEP 3: REVIEWING THE FACTORS TO BE CONSIDERED FOR EACH CRITERION ■

Once the grantwriter identifies the factors that will be considered for each criterion, he or she must determine how to compile and present the data required that will meet the criterion's requirements. By outlining the data required to respond to a specific criterion, the grantwriter will ensure that all grant components are adequately addressed. For example, a needs statement criterion for one funding proposal that provides mental health services through a school site after-school childcare program may require the following data:

(text continues on p. 90)

86   SIMPLIFIED GRANTWRITING

Form 6.1. Sample Grant Template Development Plan

Required Grant Completion Data	Specify Stakeholders and Activities Required to Complete Process	Activity Timeline
Program introduction		
Problem and needs statement • Community demographics • School district data • School site data • Participating student data		
Program design • Define goals and objectives • Create program activities with timeline		
Organizational capacity • School site's capacity • Staffing experience • Collaborators' experience		
Evaluation plan • Needs to be measured • Specific tools for measuring outcomes • Specific process plan		
Budget and budget narrative • Identify categorical costs • Identify in-kind contributions • Identify other funders • Calculate categorical totals		
Program sustainability plan • Identify future funders • Identify integrated service models • Identify subcontractors • Identify future collaborators		
Other funder requirement:		
Other funder requirement:		
Other funder requirement:		
Other funder requirement:		

Form 6.2. Evaluation Categories With Descriptions and Scoring Results

Category	Category Description	Maximum Points	Reviewer's Score
Program introduction	• Provides a brief project overview • Includes a realistic problem solution • The problem solution and project overview adequately responds to the problem Comments:	10	
Problem and needs statement	• Defines the extent of the problem • Includes community demographics and contributing factors to the problem • Impact of the problem is relevant and significant • Considers responsive program models that have a successful track record Comments:	10	
Program design	• The goals are broad statements that indicate program intent and change • Objectives are specific, measurable, attainable, related, and time sensitive • The activities and the timeline are reasonable and within the project scope Comments:	40	

(Continued)

Form 6.2. *(Continued)*

Category	Category Description	Maximum Points	Reviewer's Score
Organizational capacity	• The facility and capital equipment can support the project • The staff demonstrates adequate training, experience, and cultural sensitivity Comments:	10	
Evaluation plan	• The evaluation tools are adequate • The process plan and timeline are sufficient to effectively measure outcomes and results Comments:	20	
Budget, budget narrative, and sustainability plan	• The budget is reasonable and realistic for the services to be provided • The budget reflects sufficient program matches • The budget includes adequate in-kind contributions • The budget narrative supports the proposed budget expenditures • The program sustainability plan is reasonable for sustaining the project beyond the funding cycle Comments:	10	
	Grant proposal score	100	

Form 6.3. Category Ranges Scoring Worksheet

Category Description	Minimum Score	Average Score	Maximum Score	Reviewers' Score
Program introduction Comments:	0	5	10	
Problem and need statement Comments:	0	5	10	
Program design Comments:	0	20	40	
Organizational capacity Comments:	0	5	10	
Evaluation plan Comments:	0	10	20	
Budget, budget narrative, and sustainability plan Comments:	0	5	10	
Grant score			100	

Table 6.1 Four-Point Rubric Evaluation

4-Point Score	3-Point Score	2-Point Score	1-Point Score
Key introduction • Brief overview • Realistic solution • Responsive	Key introduction • Overview • Partially realistic • Somewhat responsive	Key introduction • Partial overview • Has a solution • Not very responsive	Key introduction • Lacks overview • Partial solution • Not responsive
Relevant problem • Defines extent • Includes demographics • Uses responsive model	Relevant problem • States extent • Some demographics • Limited model	Relevant problem • Partial extent • Few demographics • Model inadequate	Relevant problem • Extent not adequate • No model or demographics
Strong program • Broad goals • Specific objectives • Activities with timeline	Strong program • Some goals • Partial objectives • Some activities with timeline	Strong program • Partial goals • Incomplete objectives, activities, and timeline	Strong program • Incomplete goals, objectives, and timeline
Measurable evaluation • Plan is adequate and effective	Measurable evaluation • Plan is partially adequate	Measurable evaluation • Limited plan	Measurable evaluation • Not adequate or effective plan

- A description of the community including the history of the community's development, its population and ethnic composition, the average income of a household, and head of household data

- The overall health services available in the community for school-age children

- Domestic violence data and the number of foster care placements

- School district data including student graduation and drop-out rates, the number of students who have completed 4-year-college entrance requirements, and the academic achievement and literacy abilities of students

- School site data that may include the ethnic and economic composition of students, student achievement rates, school site intervention services, the number of students participating in the after-school childcare program, and the current program services

Another proposal that will provide a site-based after-school childcare tutoring and family literacy program component may request completely different data.

- The school district's current literacy and tutoring support services available to students and their families

- The school site's description of its language arts curriculum and program including the teachers' training and the students' language arts test scores

- The number of students who are limited English proficient at the school and the school's reading program that responds to these students

- The current school site's literacy intervention strategies

- The school site's reading incentive program and library services to support students and their families

When comparing the needs' criterion requirements of these two different grant proposals, it is evident that the required data to complete the proposal for a mental health service component are significantly different than the data required for a tutoring and family literacy program component. To respond to these differences, it is important to (1) clarify specifically what the grantwriter must collect to meet the funder's requirements for a specific criterion, (2) determine who should research and collect the data required for a specific criterion, and (3) decide how each grant criterion will be answered to produce the greatest impact.

STEP 4: USING SELECTION CRITERIA SCORING WEIGHTS TO PLAN THE GRANT TEMPLATE ■

The grant template should be constructed to respond to all factors that should be included in a specific criterion requirement. A grant template's layout should also be organized to provide more comprehensive information with the greatest impact focusing on grant criterion components that have higher point values. For example, the grantwriter can use a funder's evaluation score sheet to construct the grant template. If the funder requires a 10-page narrative to respond to six different criteria, the grantwriter can use the scoring point values to determine how many pages should be dedicated to respond to a particular criterion. Table 6.2 demonstrates how a grantwriter may allocate pages to respond to various criteria using scoring point values. In this example, the grantwriter has allocated a specific number of pages based on the percentage of points that can be scored for a specific criterion with the total possible score of 100 points.

Table 6.2 Number of Proposal Pages Allocated to Specific Criteria

Criterion Category	Weighted Point Score	Number of Pages Allocated to Criterion
Program introduction	10	1
Problem and needs statement	10	1
Program design	40	4
Organizational capacity	10	1
Evaluation plan	20	2
Budget, budget narrative, and sustainability plan	10	1

STEP 5: CONSTRUCTING THE GRANT TEMPLATE TO RESPOND TO SELECTION CRITERIA

All information collected to respond to a specific criterion should be tightly constructed to provide a clear, crisp, concise response that delivers a strong persuasive message to the grant reviewer. Grant templates can be designed to outline the various factors that must be addressed on the left side of the template form and provide space for various stakeholders to respond to the information required on the right side of the grant template form. Form 6.4 illustrates how a grant template can be constructed to support the data required by a funder for an after-school childcare mental health services program component. Form 6.5 exemplifies what types of information may be requested for developing a tutoring and family literacy program component. By comparing the information requested in each grant template, the grantwriter can determine how each grant template was customized to respond to a funder's specific program criteria requirements. Form 6.6 provides the grantwriter with a sample grant template.

STEP 6: ASSISTING STAKEHOLDERS IN FORMULATING GRANT RESPONSES

Once the grant template has been designed, the grantwriter can compile the requested data (1) by interviewing key stakeholders to complete

(Text continues on p. 99)

Designing a Responsive Grant Template **93**

Form 6.4. Grant Template Form for an After-School Childcare Mental Health Services Program Component

Description of Criterion Factors and Data Requested by the Funder	Criterion Factor Responses From Diverse Stakeholder Groups
Program introduction • Provide an overview of the problem. • Summarize the proposed program.	
Problem and needs statement • Report community data including health services and domestic violence statistics. • Report school district data including student population, ethnic composition, achievement data, crime statistics, and mental health support services. • Report school site data on ethnic composition and income levels, and mental health intervention services at school site.	
Program design • Goal #1: Create a comprehensive parent education program for parents. • Develop objectives, activities, and a timeline to support this goal. • Goal #2: Create student intervention counseling services for at-risk students. • Develop objectives, activities, and a timeline to support this goal.	
Organizational capacity • Describe the school's capacity to provide a confidential setting to provide services. • Describe staff training and experience. • Identify community mental health agencies that can provide specific services.	

(Continued)

Copyright © 2002 by Corwin Press, Inc. All rights reserved. Reprinted from *Simplified Grantwriting* by Mary Ann Burke. Reproduction authorized only for the local educational site or community fundraising organization that has purchased this book.

Form 6.4. (Continued)

Description of Criterion Factors and Data Requested by the Funder	Criterion Factor Responses From Diverse Stakeholder Groups
Evaluation plan • Identify or construct tools that can measure changes in parents' knowledge by participating in parent education sessions. • Identify changes in student behavior by participating in counseling sessions.	
Budget, budget narrative, and sustainability • Create a budget to support program staffing and program activities. • Create the budget narrative to explain how expenditures were determined. • Identify strategies for sustaining the program beyond the funding cycle.	

Form 6.5. Grant Template for an After-School Childcare Tutoring and Family Literacy Program Component

Description of Criterion Factors and Data Requested by the Funder	*Criterion Factor Responses From Diverse Stakeholder Groups*
Program introduction • Provide an overview of the problem. • Summarize the proposed program.	
Problem and needs statement • Report the school district's current literacy and tutoring support services. • Describe the school district's language arts curriculum and program. • Describe the teachers' training and program delivery at the school site. • Identify the number of limited English proficient students at the school and describe the program that responds to these students. • List the school's language arts test scores. • Describe the school's current literacy intervention strategies. • Describe the school site's reading incentive program and library services for students and their families.	
Program design • Goal #1: Create a student intervention tutorial program. • Develop objectives, activities, and a timeline to support this goal. • Goal #2: Create a family literacy program utilizing the school library and the reading incentive program. • Develop objectives, activities, and a timeline to support this goal.	

(Continued)

Form 6.5. (Continued)

Description of Criterion Factors and Data Requested by the Funder	Criterion Factor Responses From Diverse Stakeholder Groups
Organizational capacity • Describe the facility and the staff's training. • Describe the community agencies' services that can be provided through the program.	
Evaluation plan • Identify changes in a student's language arts performance after receiving tutoring. • Identify and construct tools that can measure parents' increased knowledge in family literacy and support for student achievement.	
Budget, budget narrative, and sustainability plan • Create the budget and plan for sustaining the program beyond the funding cycle.	

Form 6.6. Sample Grant Template

Description of Criterion Factors and Data Requested by the Funder	Criterion Factor Responses From Diverse Stakeholder Groups
Program introduction • Provide an overview of the problem. • Summarize the proposed program.	
Problem and needs statement • List and describe community and school data pertaining to the problem.	
Program design • Goal #1: • Develop objectives, activities, and a timeline to support this goal. • Goal #2: • Develop objectives, activities, and a timeline to support this goal.	
Organizational capacity • Describe the facility and the staff's training to support the program. • Describe the community agencies' services that can be provided through the program.	

(Continued)

Form 6.6. (Continued)

Description of Criterion Factors and Data Requested by the Funder	Criterion Factor Responses From Diverse Stakeholder Groups
Evaluation plan • Identify and construct tools that can measure changes in the students being served. • Determine the number of students being served in each program component. • Identify units of program services. • Describe the results that occurred because of the project and the types of evaluation instruments that were used to document the results.	
Budget, budget narrative, and sustainability plan • Create the budget and plan for sustaining the program beyond the funding cycle.	

specific criteria, (2) by circulating the template to a distribution of diverse stakeholders and having them individually complete the form, or (3) by facilitating a grant development strategic planning session with key stakeholder groups. Typically, after interviewing key stakeholders to verify that the grant template can adequately respond to the funder's criteria, it is helpful to assemble all grant development stakeholders in a strategic grantwriting session. Assembling large numbers of diverse stakeholders to create a comprehensive program grant is beneficial to the project's success for the following reasons:

1. The grantwriter has an opportunity to acquaint diverse stakeholders with the grant's requirements and receive immediate feedback on the feasibility of the project.

2. The grantwriter can leverage community support, required letters of support, and resources for the project.

3. The grantwriter can receive feedback from key stakeholders about problems within the community that should be included in the needs statement and considered in the program's design.

4. The grantwriter can receive referrals to other service providers that can provide program development support and integrative service delivery.

5. The grantwriter can determine what specific program components may best respond to the unique community needs.

6. The grantwriter can determine what facility options and staffing options would best serve the program's needs.

7. The grantwriter can accurately identify appropriate evaluation tools and processes that will support the unique needs of its school community.

8. The grantwriter can receive feedback from diverse stakeholders about appropriate expenditures and resources that can be leveraged for the program.

9. The grantwriter will receive feedback on how to sustain the project after the funding cycle is completed.

By engaging large numbers of community members in the grantwriting process, greater numbers of community groups will be able to support the project. Broad-based community support ensures that the project will receive adequate endorsement and sustained support by community empowered stakeholders.

STEP 7: EDITING DIVERSE STAKEHOLDERS'
■ GRANT TEMPLATE RESPONSES

After introducing the grant's requirements to key stakeholders, the grantwriter can organize the larger group into smaller work teams who can collectively complete a master grant template. After a specified discussion time, a group leader from each work team can report its grant template responses to the larger group. Once the strategic grant development session is completed, the grantwriter can meet with the school's leadership team to compile the school's master draft template. While working with the leadership team, the grantwriter can identify the best category responses for all stakeholders that effectively respond to the funder's grant requirements.

Once the grantwriter has met with the school, he or she can develop the first draft of the grant template. The grantwriter can also contact key informants and the evaluator to further clarify specific grant components. The grantwriter may choose to add narrative paragraphs that respond to various grant components summarized in the grant template. The grantwriter can also create individual tables for each grant category with an introductory paragraph or narrative for each section.

If several grants from various school sites within a school district are being submitted for the same grant request, the grantwriter should modify the style of each grant that will be submitted. Most funders insist that each grant should represent an original work. Many funders state that a grant will be eliminated from the review process if it was copied from another grant or has a boilerplate format. When a school district has several submissions for the same grant proposal, the funder should be contacted to clarify the following:

1. How many submissions a school district can make to remain competitive in the funding review process

2. The format options for multiple submissions

3. Whether boilerplate grant templates can be submitted from multiple sites

Once the grantwriter clarifies the format options for multiple proposal submissions, a grant template can be customized in the following ways:

- Vary the grant template's font and font size on each proposal.

- Use different word processing features on each proposal including the bold, italics, and underlining options.

- Modify the content of each grant template's subtitles and layout.

- Reorganize the information contained in the grant template and retype the narrative as a composition.

- Create a composition-style narrative and use tables to organize and highlight key data.

- Separate the boilerplate template sections and add introductory or summary paragraphs to each section.

- Create variations of different options and design new format styles for reporting key data.

When considering the customization of grant templates, the grantwriter must meet the needs of a specific funder and present the requested information in the most compelling format to ensure content clarity for program funding.

STEP 8: IDENTIFYING AND CREATING GRANT TEMPLATE EVALUATION TOOLS AND PLAN

When designing the template evaluation tools and plan, the grantwriter must identify who the evaluation stakeholders are in a particular program and determine what they believe is credible evidence for meeting a program's objectives. For example, credible evidence for a funder may be completely different from that of a school board. Evaluation tools must be developed to collect data that measure immediate results, intermediate results, and ultimate results at the end of the funding cycle. Grant template evaluation tools and a plan can be designed using the following process:

1. Create a formative evaluation plan that is designed for decision making while the program is operating.

2. Create a summative evaluation plan that is designed for decision making to determine whether a program intervention is effective and should be continued beyond the funding cycle.

3. Identify what types of data should be collected to support formative or summative evaluation results. Examples of school- and district-level data include standardized test scores, student achievement data, report card data, and attendance data; the numbers of students receiving different types of intervention services; the incidence of school truancy, dropout rates, and graduation rates; the number of students completing 4-year-college entrance requirements; the number of limited English proficient students; the number of students who are from low-income families and qualify for free and reduced lunches; the number of students living in foster care or in out-of-placement homes; the number of teen pregnancies; and the number of students involved in specific crimes.

4. In addition to specific data that are available at school sites and district offices, the grantwriter can create data collection instruments that can compile other types of data. Instruments that can support the collection of data include various types of tests, in-depth interviews, survey forms, questionnaire forms, focus groups, and telephone interviews. Tests, questionnaires, and surveys can be constructed to measure changes in knowledge, behavior, perceptions, beliefs, attitudes, and values.

5. Before creating an evaluation plan, the grantwriter must first determine what specific results the funder desires to achieve from a proposed program, what the program participants intend to achieve, and what the fiscal agent or school intends to achieve. It is not uncommon that each group has different perceptions and agendas about what results and program components are more important to achieve. With further discussion, all stakeholders can prioritize and clarify a holistic problem solution that best meets the needs of a specific student population.

6. The grantwriter should use the advisory services of an outside program auditor or evaluations consultant from a local college or university who has an extensive research and program development background. This consultant can be used to initially check the evaluation design and tools for measurement, as well as check the completion of the evaluation plan at the end of the funding cycle. For smaller grants, university professors and research institute directors can be hired for a 2-day consultation fee. It is also not uncommon to use an outside consultant for designing the evaluation plan and completing the evaluation for large federal and foundation grants that exceed annual budgets of $500,000. Consultant fees for these services vary widely and should be considered when creating the project budget.

Form 6.7 provides a sample evaluation template for the grantwriter to use in creating an evaluation grant template plan that can support the various stakeholders' outcome priorities. Once the grantwriter determines each stakeholder's prioritized need, the grantwriter can create an evaluation plan with appropriate instruments that can generate credible evidence.

STEP 9: SECURING FEEDBACK FROM ■ STAKEHOLDERS FOR COMPLETING THE GRANT

Once the grantwriter has completed the grant template, he or she should convene a grant development review team consisting of the following individuals:

Form 6.7. Sample Evaluation Template

Stakeholder Group	List Each Objective With Anticipated Results	Identify Evaluation Tools and Plan
Funder		
School district		
School		
Community agencies		
Students		
Parents		
Other		
Other		
Other		

1. A central office administrator who must sign off for the grant submission

2. The school site principal who will be responsible for the grant

3. Representatives from the school's leadership team who will be responsible for the program's implementation and evaluation

4. A representative from personnel who will be responsible for hiring program staff

5. A representative from the district's fiscal services department who will be responsible for approving the budget and any subcontractor contracts

6. An outside program auditor or evaluator from an institute of higher education if the grantwriter has chosen to use this type of support or if the funder requests these services

7. Any community-based organizations or subcontractors who will provide various program components

8. Any other school site staff, school district office personnel, or group who will be responsible for various program components

During a grant development review, the team should review the grant for accuracy and responsiveness in addressing the funder's requirements. All team members should ask clarification questions to determine if the various grant components are clearly explained and described. The grantwriter should list any areas of concern for further grant development. Additionally, the grantwriter must work with the team in creating a responsive and realistic budget that adequately supports the proposed program and responds to the funder's budget requirements. Finally, the team should determine how the proposed program could sustain itself beyond the funding cycle.

STEP 10: DESIGNING A TEMPLATE BUDGET, BUDGET NARRATIVE, AND SUSTAINABILITY PLAN

The budget, budget narrative, and sustainability plan grant template should be constructed to (1) meet the funding requirements of the funder, and (2) clarify all budget expenditures and supporting financial information that have been requested.

There are a variety of budget formats used by funders including the simplified line-item budget by category displayed in Form 5.6, a functional program budget that reports only revenues and expenses related to a specific program, and the total organizational budget that reports all revenues and expenses for the entire school or organization. Other budget formats may include a column for in-kind contributions or for anticipated funding from other sources. Budget format variations for these budget types are expansive.

When constructing grant budget templates that modify standard budget formats, the grantwriter's primary focus should be to simplify the reporting of the financial data requested by the funder. Form 5.6, Table 5.11, and Form 5.8 in Chapter 5 illustrate how to design effective budget models for organizing and reporting critical financial data in a program budget, budget narrative, and program sustainability plan.

STEP 11: CREATING A FOLLOW-UP TEMPLATE PLAN ■

Once the grant is completed, the grantwriter should check all grant components for completeness and determine if the grant requires a cover letter, any attachments, or other forms that must be signed and submitted with the grant proposal. The deadline for submission and the actual address that the grant should be mailed to also should be verified. Many funders request that a grant identification number be referenced on the grant proposal's envelope. Some funders require that the grant applicant complete specific mailing procedures and secure documentation that the grant proposal was mailed by a specific time and date.

During this review of final submission requirements, the grantwriter should create a plan that will document and track any follow-up activities required after the grant is mailed for submission. The grantwriter will want to contact the funder after funding decisions are made and should verify how funding decisions will be communicated to applicants. Many government funders initially post grant funding recommendations on the funders' Web site and follow up with a mailing of the grant award letter or grant contract notification letter. Many grant contract letters require signatures and forms to be completed within 10 days of notification. The grantwriter should also review any grant compliance reporting that will be required throughout the project's duration. Grant compliance requirements for new grant applicants can include quarterly program implementation and units of service reporting and quarterly budget expenditure reporting. Many government funders provide regional training sessions on how to complete all grant implementation and reporting requirements.

Occasionally, grant awards are significantly reduced and applicants are required to resubmit a revised program plan and budget. When grant awards are significantly cut, it is critical for the grantwriter to contact the funder and renegotiate how the program should be implemented to meet the funder's requirements and to create a viable program that will serve the unique program needs of the applicant. Sometimes, when renegotiating a program plan due to reduced budget allocations, the applicant determines that the project would not be feasible or beneficial for program implementation. At that point, the funder must assist the grant applicant in determining how subcontractors can support part of the program's needs.

Form 6.8 provides a sample grant follow-up template plan that the grantwriter can use to identify key events, responsible individuals, and timelines for completing the grant submission, grant award notification, grant acceptance, and grant implementation program reporting requirements.

Form 6.8. Sample Grant Follow-Up Template Plan

Timeline and Deadline	*Responsible Individual*	*Description of Follow-Up Activity*
		Submission requirements and schedule:
		Grant award notification and assurance sign-off schedule and process:
		Interim program reporting schedule and form requirements:
		Interim budget expenditure reporting schedule and form requirements:
		Program implementation funder training schedule and activities:
		Program implementation site visits and technical support meeting schedule and activities:
		Final reporting requirements:

7

Modifying Program Proposals to Meet Diverse Funders' Needs

Once a critical program need has been included in a grant proposal, additional funding sources can be identified to add more resources or to support a specific need. It is appropriate to seek funds from more than one source at a time once the initial funding has been awarded and modifications in the program delivery have been adjusted through the funder for effective implementation. Various strategies a school or district can use to leverage added program funding and resources include the following:

- Identifying other funders who can provide additional support or who can expand services

- Identifying other community resources that can provide other program components

- Identifying funding or community partners who can expand services in a new service area with the school or the district

- Cross-selling the program to others who may know prospective funders or resources

- Creating an expansive public relations program to heighten the project's visibility and garner community support for added resources

Once a school or district identifies added funding sources to expand or to add supplementary program services, the grantwriter can modify and create different versions of the original grant proposal template to respond to the new funder's requirements using the following process:

1. The grantwriter should review the new funder's proposal requirements and compare the new grant's requirements to the original grant template.

2. If most of the grant components and information requested by the new funder is similar to the original grant template, the grantwriter can edit the original grant template and modify and add information where required. The grantwriter can also create a one-page letter of solicitation, and a three- to five-page program overview letter of solicitation to submit to foundation funders for preliminary review.

3. If the grant content information from the new funder is radically different from the original funder's template, then the grantwriter can create a new grant template form using the process described in Chapter 6.

4. The grantwriter can transfer relevant data from the original template to meet new content requirements in the new grant template.

5. The intent in developing the new grant template is to clearly articulate what has happened in the program based on the original grant request and the program's implementation to date. It is far easier to leverage more funding for an existing program than to generate seed funding for a new program. With this concept in mind, the grantwriter must tell the story of how the existing program is making a difference and impact in the lives of its students by using a specific intervention strategy or problem solution.

6. As described in Chapter 6, the grantwriter must reassemble the grant development review team from the district office, the school site, the institute of higher education, and the community agencies involved in the project to review the newly developed grant and to create a new budget reflecting the resources required for the newly expanded program component.

7. A new follow-up plan must be developed to track the funding review process and plan for program implementation.

The grantwriter may also decide to apply to multiple funders for various program components at the same time. Tips for effective coordination and solicitation include the following:

- Creating a grant-tracking database of all grant submissions for various grant components with a timeline of the decision-making process for each grant proposal submitted

- Identifying and prioritizing which program components must be implemented first to maximize and streamline service delivery

- Specifying the various program funders for specific program services, the pending program funders for new or expanded services, and the proposed funders in a program sustainability plan for future funding and program expansion

- Contacting existing funders to inform them about any program modifications or additional services provided by new funding sources

- Providing existing funders with the opportunity to further fund new program components

- Maintaining ongoing communications with all current funding sources and with prospective funders who may seek successful programs for further investment

The grantwriter should review all previous chapters to determine how the school or district can leverage added or new program resources. Using the after-school childcare example displayed throughout the book, Tables 7.1 through 7.3 illustrate how a grantwriter can create a matrix of options to fund and integrate various funders' requirements to maximize service delivery and program results. Table 7.1 provides a worksheet that can help a school or district identify the various program components for added funding. Table 7.2 provides a matrix of funding options that a school or school district can use for determining which program components could be funded by different funding sources. Table 7.3 provides a worksheet that a grantwriter can use for creating an integrated funding plan.

Table 7.1 Sample After-School Childcare Program Component Identification Worksheet

Currently Funded Program Component	
Component	*Description and Funder*
Childcare	Monday through Friday on-site childcare services are provided from 3 p.m. until 6 p.m. to a total of 200 low-income primarily K-3 students through a contract with the We Care Child Development Agency and funded through a 21st Century Federal Grant.
Nutritional snack	Monday through Friday on-site nutritional snacks are provided at 3:30 p.m. to a total of 200 low-income primarily K-3 students through a contract with the We Care Child Development Agency, funded through a 21st Century Federal Grant.
Tutoring	Tutoring is provided by the Academic Partners Volunteer Tutoring Agency and funded through a federal AmeriCorps Grant.
Mental health services	Mental health individual counseling services are provided by a licensed clinical social worker on Wednesdays by appointment through a contract with Let's Help Counseling Agency and funded through a Solutions Community Foundation Grant.
Proposed New Program Components Requiring Funding	
Component	*Description/Funding Options*
Organized sports	Monday through Friday organized soccer, basketball, and baseball teams can be funded by federal, state, and community foundation grants.
Performing arts	Monday through Friday performing arts activities including drama, dance, singing, and stage production can be funded by college, state, federal, and community grants.

Table 7.2 Sample After-School Childcare Program Matrix of Funding Options

Funder	Childcare	Snacks	Tutoring	Sports	Arts
21st Century Learning Center Federal Grant	✓	✓	✓	✓	✓
AmeriCorps State Grant			✓		
Reading Excellence Act State Grant			✓		
School Safety and After-School Partnership State Grants	✓	✓	✓	✓	✓
Community foundations	✓	✓	✓	✓	✓
School district food services program		✓			
Community Police Activity League				✓	
Community theater groups					✓
Colleges and universities			✓	✓	✓
Corporate sponsors	✓	✓	✓	✓	✓

Table 7.3 Sample After-School Childcare Program Integrated Funding Plan Worksheet

Currently Funded Program Component	
Component	*Funder and Possible Added Sources*
Childcare	Funded by 21st Century Federal Grant Could leverage added funding from the School Safety and After-School Partnership Grants, community foundations, and corporate sponsors.
Nutritional snack	Funded by 21st Century Federal Grant Could leverage added funding from the School Safety and After-School Partnership State Grants, community foundations, corporate sponsors, and the school district.
Tutoring	Funded by federal AmeriCorps Grant Could leverage added funding from the 21st Century Federal Grant, the School Safety and After-School Partnership State Grants, community foundations, colleges and universities, and corporate sponsors.
Mental health services	This service was not considered for other funding options due to the services being provided from a community agency performing satellite program services at the school site.
Proposed New Program Components Requiring Funding	
Component	*Proposed Funding Source Options*
Organized sports	*Funding could be provided through the 21st Century Learning Center Federal Grant, the School Safety and After-School Partnership State Grants, the Community Police Activity League, colleges and universities, and corporate sponsors.
Performing arts	*Funding could be provided through the 21st Century Learning Center Federal Grant, the School Safety and After-School Partnership State Grants, community theater groups, colleges and universities, and corporate sponsors.

NOTE: *When evaluating the various proposed funding options for the organized sports program component and for the performing arts program component, the grantwriter should first use funding with the greatest limitations in flexible spending. In this example, the Community Police Activity League will only fund the organized sports program component and the community theater groups will only fund performing arts programs. After using the funding available from these two limited funding sources, the grantwriter can leverage funding from any of the other sources that all have the potential of funding both program components.

8

Establishing a Program Sustainability Plan for Continuous Support

Establishing an integrative program sustainability plan allows school site programs to become institutionalized service delivery program models within a school or school district. Form 8.1 contains a long-range fundraising plan worksheet to assist educational practitioners in strategically evaluating all current programs being funded by diverse funders. It also helps identify any overlaps in service delivery or need for added services. Through this strategic planning tool, schools and districts can effectively plan for future programs and determine funding needs. Strategic integrative program delivery allows school districts to maximize their resource utilization to equitably support the diverse learning needs of their student populations.

After a school site identifies all funder options and the specific types of funding for its many programs, the school and school district can follow the grantwriting and fund development process described in this book. This process includes the following simplified activities:

- Identifying funders for strategic planning for program development
- Creating marketing strategies for leveraging program funding
- Integrating program collaborations

Form 8.1. Sample Long-Range Fundraising Plan Worksheet

Program Name	Funder Options/Specific Type of Funding Source		
	Federal	State	*Other

NOTE: *Other includes funding from regional, county, local, private foundation, corporate sponsorship, and other funding sources.

- Designing effective organizational and time management strategies
- Constructing integral grant proposal components
- Designing a responsive grant template plan with customization features
- Modifying grant proposals to meet diverse funders' needs
- Establishing a long-term sustainability plan for continuous support

By following this disciplined process of grant development activities, a school can be assured that its collaborative grantwriting team is provided with the essential tools to create a systematic seamless delivery system of services. A streamlined system can be productive, efficient, and responsive in meeting the unique learning needs of students in its school community. The results of various service provider collaborative teams have the capacity to impress funders with their sophistication and creativity in continuing to challenge the traditional methods of service delivery and funding. These innovative partnerships continue to produce outcomes that can better serve the school community's educational needs and extended health and human care support services.

Suggested Readings

Anderson, K. (1981). *Cutting deals with unlikely allies: An unorthodox approach to playing the political game.* Berkeley, CA: Anderson Negotiations/Communications Press.

Brewer, E. W., Achilles, C. M., Fuhriman, J. R., & Hollingsworth, C. (2001). *Finding funding.* Thousand Oaks, CA: Corwin.

Burke, J., & Prater, C. A. (2000). *I'll grant you that.* Westport, CT: Greenwood Heinemann.

Burke, M. A., & Liljenstolpe, C. (1993). *Creative fund-raising.* Menlo Park, CA: Crisp.

Burke, M. A., & Picus, L. O. (2001). *Developing community empowered schools.* Thousand Oaks, CA: Corwin.

Coley, S. M., & Scheinberg, C. A. (2000). *Proposal writing.* Thousand Oaks, CA: Sage.

Fullan, M. (1993). *Change forces.* Bristol, PA: Falmer.

Geever, J. C., & McNeill, P. (1993). *The foundation center's guide to proposal writing.* New York: Foundation Center.

Grills, C. N., Bass, K., Brown, D. L., & Akers, A. (1996). Empowerment evaluation: Building upon a tradition of activism in the African American community. In D. M. Fetterman, S. K. Kaftarian, & A. Wandersman (Eds.), *Empowerment evaluation: Knowledge and tools for self-assessment and accountability* (pp. 123-140). Thousand Oaks, CA: Sage.

Hall, M. S. (1988). *Getting funded: A complete guide to proposal writing.* Portland, OR: Continuing Education Publications, Portland State University.

Hanushek, E. A. (1994). *Making schools work.* Washington, DC: Brookings Institution.

Herman, J. L., & Winters, L. (1992). *Tracking your school's success.* Newbury Park, CA: Corwin.

Holcomb, E. L. (1999). *Getting excited about data.* Thousand Oaks, CA: Corwin.

Levin, H. M., & McEwan, P. (2001). *Cost-effectiveness analysis: Methods and applications.* Thousand Oaks, CA: Corwin.

Lindsey, R. B., Nuri-Robins, K., & Terrell, R. D. (1999). *Cultural proficiency.* Thousand Oaks, CA: Corwin.

Locke, L. F., Spirduso, W. W., & Silverman, S. J. (1999). *Proposals that work.* Thousand Oaks, CA: Sage.

Mahon, L. (1997). *A grantseeker manual.* Millbrae, CA: Trident Enterprises.

Marzano, R. J. (2001). *Designing a new taxonomy of educational objectives.* Thousand Oaks, CA: Corwin.

Oakes, J., Quartz, K. H., Ryan, S., & Lipton, M. (2000). *Becoming good American schools.* San Francisco, CA: Jossey-Bass.

Odden, A., & Archibald, S. (2001). *Reallocating resources: How to boost student achievement without asking for more.* Thousand Oaks, CA: Corwin.

Peterson, S. (2001). *The grantwriter's Internet companion.* Thousand Oaks, CA: Corwin.

Picus, L. O. (2001). *In search of more productive schools: A guide to resource allocation in education.* Eugene, OR: ERIC Clearinghouse on Educational Management.

Ramsey, R. D. (2001). *Fiscal fitness for school administrators: How to stretch resources and do even more for less.* Thousand Oaks, CA: Corwin.

Sanders, E. T. W. (1999). *Urban school leadership: Issues and strategies.* Larchmont, NY: Eye on Education.

Speck, M., & Knipe, C. (2001). *Why can't we get it right?* Thousand Oaks, CA: Corwin.

U. S. Department of Education. (1998). *What should I know about ED grants?* Washington, DC: U. S. Department of Education Grants Policy and Oversight Staff.

Williams, H. S., Webb, A. Y., & Phillips, W. J. (1991). *Outcome funding: A new approach to targeted grantmaking.* Rensselaerville, NY: Rensselaerville Institute.

Index

CORWIN
PRESS

The Corwin Press logo—a raven striding across an open book—represents the happy union of courage and learning. We are a professional-level publisher of books and journals for K-12 educators, and we are committed to creating and providing resources that embody these qualities. Corwin's motto is "Success for All Learners."